SOUTHERN
BAKED

CELEBRATING LIFE WITH PIE

·····················

SOUTHERN BAKED

·····················

AMANDA DALTON WILBANKS

Photographs by Gill Autrey

GIBBS SMITH
TO ENRICH AND INSPIRE HUMANKIND

First Edition
22 21 20 19 18   5 4 3 2

Published by
Gibbs Smith
P.O. Box 667
Layton, Utah 84041

1.800.835.4993 orders
www.gibbs-smith.com

Designed by Rita Sowins / Sowins Design
Printed in China

Gibbs Smith books are printed on either recycled, 100% post-consumer waste,
FSC-certified papers or on paper produced from sustainable PEFC-certified forest/
controlled wood source. Learn more at www.pefc.org.

Library of Congress Cataloging-in-Publication Data

Names: Wilbanks, Amanda Dalton, author.
Title: Southern baked : celebrating life with pie / Amanda Dalton Wilbanks.
Description: First edition. | Layton, Utah : Gibbs Smith, [2018] | Includes index.
Identifiers: LCCN 2018000352 | ISBN 9781423648987 (hardcover)
Subjects: LCSH: Pies. | LCGFT: Cookbooks.
Classification: LCC TX773 .W63 2018 | DDC 641.8⁶/52--dc23 LC record
available at https://lccn.loc.gov/2018000352

TO MY HUSBAND ALEX, I HAVE SO
MANY REASONS TO CELEBRATE
BECAUSE OF YOU. I LOVE YOU!

CONTENTS

INTRODUCTION

GROWING UP, I NEVER THOUGHT I'D BE A PIE BAKER. A COOK, MAYBE, BUT NOT A BAKER.

After all, my culinary role models were stellar. Growing up in the South, I was always a hands-on cook, raised in my mother's and grandmothers' kitchens, rolling out biscuit dough and stirring aromatic pots over the stove, shelling peas, and canning bounty from our garden. The hustle and bustle of it all was like a second language to me—one that involved touch and taste and smell as much as it did sound or sight. Then, when we all met around the table to enjoy the fruits of our labor, I felt connected to my family on a deeper level. I knew from a young age that food was my favorite way of saying, "I love you."

Farm-to-table is a trendy expression; yet, in my small town, that's the way it was. Everybody had a garden, or at least access to one. We grew the food we ate and ate the food we grew. If I close my eyes, I can still feel the Georgia heat on my neck as I sat on grandmother's screened porch, stringing beans straight from the garden while we chatted about a friend's needs or the latest news, or humming to fill the quiet spaces. Whether it be after church on Sunday for lunch, or while dropping off a homemade casserole at a friend's house who just had a baby, in the South, we take time to savor the moment and truly celebrate our friendships, our love, our labor, or even a passing.

Cooking with fresh ingredients and no shortcuts is a ritual in my family, passed down from my grandmothers, to my mother, to me. They taught me that delicious doesn't mean difficult, and that the best flavors come from simple, natural ingredients mixed with lots of care. When I met and married my husband Alex, I learned these values could also be applied to dessert through his mother—my precious mother-in-law Sandy!

It was Sandy who expanded my cooking horizons by teaching me how to make my first "scratch pie." I can still remember how anxious I was when, while visiting our home from far-away Colorado, she suggested we make Alex's favorite buttermilk pie. I watched her gather the butter, sugar, flour, and eggs, and then expertly mix them together. I could see in every movement that baking was an act of love for her, just like other types of cooking were for me. By the time the pie came out of the oven, I felt more connected to her than ever.

That single buttermilk pie, the sweetest thing I'd ever smelled, started a personal revolution for me. Before long I was baking pies all the time. Alex and I must have each gained ten pounds that summer eating pie. Soon, he issued an ultimatum: either stop baking or get those pies out of our house!

The next logical step was to bake my pies for friends and neighbors, who urged me to share them with a wider audience by selling them. My first attempt at being "a pie lady" was at the annual Mule Camp Festival, held every October in my town, Gainesville, Georgia. I borrowed a tent, created a business name and logo, printed up 1000 business cards (every one of which was given away that weekend), had a banner made, fashioned a Facebook page, baked scores of pies, and recruited my family to help. I didn't sleep for thirty-six hours straight, but it was worth the gamble. The inaugural weekend was a raging success. Southern Baked Pie Company was born.

I continued with more of Sandy's recipes, adding in those from other family members, eventually feeling confident enough to make up my own.

I was in love, not only with the process of making pies, but with the way they connected people. Pies are meant to be shared. Whether it's between families, friends, or even acquaintances, pie brings us together. In fact, it was Jane Austen who said, "Good apple pies are a considerable part of our domestic happiness." Jane was right!

I was inspired to open Southern Baked Pie Company by this simple mission: to create something that made people happy. Our company motto became "Celebrate Life with Pie!" because our pies make virtually everyone smile. Each pie, sweet or savory, is a tasty jewel at any life celebration, even one as mundane and sacred as the family dinner table.

As much as I love to bake pies, I also enjoy teaching people how to follow in my footsteps. The art of making a flaky, melt-in-your-mouth crust, or a filling so good it makes people weak in the knees, isn't as intimidating as it seems. Trust me, if I can do it, anyone can.

That's why I've been teaching pie-baking classes out of the Southern Baked kitchen for the past few years now. I love to see the look on people's faces when they realize how easy "from scratch" baking is. Likewise, it is so affirming to hear from people who felt inspired to go back home and try my recipes with their friends and family.

When approached about doing this book I was ecstatic to have the chance to combine my twin passions for cooking and pie making. Not only that, this book is another opportunity to show people that pies belong on every table, not just the dessert table, and to demonstrate the joy a homemade meal can bring to our days. Baking and cooking are such simple pleasures. They can mean so much to you and the people around you.

Delicious meals are a tradition in my family, as much as the tradition of mothers working outside the home. Even as a full-time working mother, I try to pass on the precious gifts I've received in the kitchen to my children each night when I get home from work. I want my sons to feel as connected to cooking as I do. But because my days are busy, I also don't want to spend hours slaving over a stove after a long day at the pie shop.

That's why the recipes in this book are tried-and-true. Tested again and again in my own kitchen to be easy, beautiful, and flavorful, inspired by everything from old-fashioned Southern family recipes, to cooking shows, to the places I've been lucky enough to travel to over the years; each recipe is guaranteed to be a pure delight.

Because I enjoy incorporating unexpected flavors for mouth-watering results, you'll find flavor-packed recipes like Roma Tomato Tart (page 46), Paradise Soup (page 85), and Lemon Chess Pie (page 39) in this book. These dishes are just as perfect for a "dinner in" as they are for a tailgate. Although the recipes are organized chronologically by the months of the year and are tied to seasonal events, don't be afraid to mix and match your favorites!

Good cooking is both an art and a legacy. Through these timeless recipes and celebrations, I am able to share with you traditions that have made my family's life richer and more bountiful. It's my hope they will be embraced and enjoyed by your family for generations as well.

SOUTHERN BAKED PIE DOUGH

Sandy Wilbanks, my mother-in-law, taught me to make pie dough for the first time. With less than five ingredients, she showed me how to make one of the most versatile and delicious pastries I have ever made. Little did I know at the time, but the basic recipe would become the star of every pie I made, and eventually become the basis for all the pies produced by my company. At Southern Baked Pie Company, we are famous for our buttery, flakey crust. It will literally melt in your mouth. To me, the crust is the best part—the filling is just fluff. I could eat our Southern Baked Pie Dough raw, baked with cinnamon and sugar, or cut into shapes, baked, and enjoyed as cookies with a hot cup of coffee. My Southern Baked Pie Dough recipe (page 17) can be used for both sweet and savory dishes and pies. The sky is the limit with what you can create. Enjoy!

SOUTHERN BAKED PIE DOUGH (SB PIE DOUGH)

8 tablespoons (1 stick) unsalted butter

1 1/4 cups all-purpose flour

1/2 teaspoon salt

1/2 teaspoon granulated sugar

1/4 cup water

Cut the butter into small cubes. Combine butter and flour in a mixing bowl. Using a pastry blender, work the butter into the flour. Add the salt and sugar. Continue to work the butter into the flour until the mixture has a consistency of course-ground cornmeal. The cubes of butter should now be smaller than the size of a green pea.

Add the water, all at once. Continue to work the dough until the dough begins to come together. Form the dough into a ball, wrap with plastic wrap, and press into the shape of a disk. Place in the refrigerator for 2 hours to chill.

Remove dough from refrigerator and roll out to desired size on a lightly floured surface.

Tip: The trick to making delicious pie dough is using cold ingredients. I even chill my flour, salt, and sugar. Starting with very cold butter and ice cold water will make a world of difference when it comes to the texture of the dough.

PIE DOUGH TIPS

All ingredients must be cold! I even refrigerate my flour to chill it before I begin working. And make sure to add ice cubes to the water to ensure it is ice cold.

You want the ingredients to form dough that isn't too sticky. Be careful and don't add too much water.

Handle the dough as little as possible. The more you work and handle it, the warmer the ingredients get.

Roll out dough between two pieces of parchment paper to avoid making a floury mess in the kitchen.

When rolling out the dough, roll from the center to the edges. Then quarter turn the dough and roll from the center and back out to the edge again. Continue quarter turning the dough and repeating this process until a nice, even circle is formed.

If dough is sticky when rolling, lightly sprinkle with flour.

Always roll pie dough to a 1/8-inch thickness.

Disks of dough can be refrigerated for up to two days if you need to make the dough ahead of time. Wrap the disks with plastic wrap before refrigerating.

You can also freeze the pie dough. I like to make a couple of recipes of dough at a time, roll them out, place in pie plates, flute, and then store in the freezer for up to 6 months. Wrap the dough-filled pie plates with plastic wrap and cover with aluminum foil to prevent freezer burn. It's always nice to have a pie crust on hand when you are in a rush and don't have time to make one.

PREBAKED DOUGH

A prebaked dough means that the dough is fully cooked, and is used when the filling of a pie recipe will not be baked. An example is a coconut cream pie.

I recipe SB Pie Dough (page 17)

Preheat oven to 375 degrees.

Roll out dough to desired size and place in pie plate or tart pan. Dock (prick) the dough with a fork on the bottom and up the sides of the plate. Place in freezer for 30 minutes before baking. This helps set the dough.

Remove dough from freezer and line the inside of the dough with parchment paper, completely covering the dough. Fill the pie plate with dried beans. This will ensure that the dough maintains its shape.

Bake for 12–15 minutes. Remove the beans and parchment and return pie plate to the oven and bake for 15–20 minutes, or until golden brown. Let cool completely before adding a filling.

PARTIALLY BAKED DOUGH

Partially baked dough is used for recipes that require less than 30 minutes baking time—the raw pie dough doesn't have enough time to fully cook, ultimately resulting in a soggy-bottom crust. To eliminate this, partially bake the dough.

I recipe SB Pie Dough (page 17)

Preheat oven to 375 degrees.

Roll out dough to desired size and place in pie plate or tart pan. Dock (prick) the dough with a fork on the bottom and up the sides of the plate. Place in freezer for 30 minutes before baking. This helps set the dough.

Remove dough from freezer and line the inside of the dough with parchment paper, completely covering the dough. Fill the pie plate with dried beans. This will ensure that the dough maintains its shape while baking.

Bake for 12–15 minutes. Remove the beans and parchment. Set on counter to cool.

LATTICE TOP PIE

Here are some helpful hints and suggestions for making a lattice top pie. It takes patience and some time, but the beautiful pie you create is so worth it. I challenge you to get creative with your lattice and weaving. Most importantly, celebrate and have fun!

Dough can't be cold for latticing, so make sure to let the dough come to room temperature before rolling out and cutting strips. If the dough feels sticky, sprinkle with just a little bit of flour.

Roll out dough to a 12 inch circle. Cut 1-inch-thick strips with a pastry cutter that has a fluted wheel. You should get approximately 8 to 10 strips. When making a lattice crust, it's important to start in the middle of the pie crust. Lay the longest strip in the center of the pie, on top of the filling. Then take two more strips and place on either side of the middle strip. Repeat again. Then take every other strip and fold half way to the other side of the pie. Place a strip in the middle, perpendicular to all the other strips. Fold the strips back over the newly placed dough strip. Repeat this process, picking up every other dough strip and folding back, laying a new strip of dough perpendicular to the other, and then folding the dough strips back over across the newly placed strip of dough until top is completely latticed, working your way from the center out. You are essentially making a "t" or cross with the strips of dough.

To make a very tight lattice crust (like the one pictured) with no space in between the dough strips, you will need to roll out two recipes of SB Pie Dough (page 17). Cut each dough circle into tiny strips, about 1/2 inch thick. Then begin to weave the strips together, starting by pulling back every other strip across the center, and then taking the strips from the additional dough and weaving together using the same process as above. I find it helpful to do this on a piece of parchment paper then carefully lift the latticed crust to the top of the pie.

JANUARY
New Year's Day Dinner

At my house, New Year's has always been a mix of tradition and innovation. Since New Year's Eve is typically a night filled with parties, drinks, and friends, I like to scale it back a notch on New Year's Day and create a relaxed, comforting meal to enjoy with my family. I love taking the opportunity to honor the old Southern customs, like eating collard greens and black-eyed peas to usher in a year of health, wealth, and good fortune. But, I also treasure the opportunity to try new recipes, make new memories, and look toward the future. New Year's is such a unique holiday—perfect for combining classic recipes with creative, unexpected flavors. Serve these dishes for a giant New Year's feast, or a quiet night in with the family. Either way, they'll have people in just the right mood to usher in a new beginning.

Apple-Raisin Tarts with Sabayon Cream

Chicken Dumpling Pie

Spicy Southern Collards

Black-Eyed Pea Salad with Hot Bacon Dressing

Skillet Cornbread

Lemon Chess Pie

APPLE-RAISIN TARTS WITH SABAYON CREAM

SERVES 8

Inspired by a rustic French apple tart, these rich, warm tarts are a cold weather twist on an everyday favorite dessert in my household. Hints of nutmeg and cinnamon give flavor and warmth, while a generous kick of rum adds just the right festive touch.

I cup raisins

1/4 cup rum

2 recipes SB Pie Dough (page 17)

3 Granny Smith apples

2 Golden Delicious apples

I teaspoon lemon juice

2 tablespoons brown sugar

1/8 teaspoon nutmeg

2 tablespoons granulated sugar

3 tablespoons butter, cut into small cubes

I cup apricot jam

I teaspoon vanilla

Preheat oven to 400 degrees. Soak raisins in rum while preparing the tarts.

Roll out the dough into 2 (12-inch) circles. Cut 4 (5-inch) circles out of each round to make 8 in total. Mold into individual (4-inch) round tart pans.

Peel apples, cut in half, and remove core and stems. Cut apples into 1/4-inch slices. Place in a bowl and toss with lemon juice; set aside.

Sprinkle the bottom of each tart shell with brown sugar. Arrange apples, overlapping in a circular pattern, in the tart pans. Mix nutmeg and sugar together and sprinkle over the apples. Dot tops with butter. Place tart pans on a parchment-lined baking sheet and bake for 40 minutes.

Heat jam, vanilla, and rum with soaked raisins in a small saucepan. Bring just to a boil. Remove from heat and spoon over the top of the tarts. Serve hot with Sabayon Cream, homemade whipped cream, or vanilla ice cream.

continued

Sabayon Cream

MAKES APPROXIMATELY 1 CUP

Sabayon is a light custard sauce, typically made with egg yolks, sugar, and a sweet wine, served with fruit desserts or by itself. You can slightly change the flavor of the cream by substituting different types of wine. Try a dry white or a sparkling wine.

> 1 egg
> 2 egg yolks
> 1/2 cup granulated sugar
> 1/3 cup Marsala or bourbon
> 1/3 cup dry white French vermouth

Combine all ingredients in a stainless steel saucepan and cook over low heat for 4–5 minutes, whisking slowly until cream has thickened and is foamy and warm to the touch. Let come to room temperature and then chill until ready to serve.

CHICKEN DUMPLING PIE

SERVES 8

This dish reminds me so much of my grandmother, Betty Dalton. When I was a little girl, she told me I could call her Betty, because grandmother simply sounded too old. A prim, proper, and strikingly beautiful southern lady she was—never frazzled in the kitchen. She moved with a lightness in her steps, always calm and graceful as she cooked. She would make this every time extended family came down to visit from Lexington, Kentucky. It's warm, buttery pastry crust, soft dumpling filling, and rich chicken flavor makes everyone feel at home. Serve with warm homemade chicken broth on the side, as some prefer a juicier filling.

2 cups all-purpose flour

1/2 cup self-rising flour

1 teaspoon salt

4 tablespoons canola oil

1/4 cup hot water

1 whole roasted chicken

Freshly ground black pepper, to taste

3 quarts chicken broth

1 recipe SB Pie Dough (page 17)

Preheat oven to 300 degrees.

Mix both flours, salt, oil, and water together in a bowl to make a dough. On a lightly floured surface, roll out dough to 1/4-inch thickness and cut into 1/2-inch strips for the dumplings. Set aside.

Pull the meat off the chicken, cut into bite-size pieces, and spread 1/3 of the chicken in the bottom of a Dutch oven; sprinkle with pepper, and cover with 1/3 of the strips of dough. Cover with 1/3 of the broth. Add another layer of chicken, sprinkle with black pepper, and cover with strips of dough. Float with 1/3 of the broth. Finish with final layer of chicken, pepper, dough strips, and remaining broth.

Roll out dough large enough to cover the Dutch oven and place over top, leaving the dough edges rough. The dough may sink down into the broth, but it will rise up as the pie bakes. Freeze for 1 hour.

Bake in the bottom third of the oven for 1 1/2 hours or until crust is golden brown.

SPICY SOUTHERN COLLARDS

SERVES 6

In the South it's considered a homemade sin if you don't eat your collards on New Year's because they signify "green" money. For fear that I won't be blessed with any money in the coming year; I've always eaten as big a bowl as possible. Whether the old Southern tale is true or not, I do believe eating collards is a great way to add a little extra luck to your New Year's celebration and the year ahead. Cut the leaves into ribbons to reduce cooking time, and amp up the flavor with some rich fatback and spicy red pepper flakes for a dish that no one will be able to resist.

3 bunches collard greens

1 tablespoon olive oil

2 tablespoons butter

1 medium onion, chopped

1/2 tablespoon red pepper flakes

4 cloves garlic, chopped

2 small strips of streak o' lean (salt pork or fatback)

1 1/2 quarts chicken broth

Wash collards and let dry.

Heat oil and butter in a large Dutch oven. Sauté onion until translucent and add red pepper flakes.

Prepare the greens by removing the stems. Lay the leaves on top of one another and roll up like a cigar to cut the leaves into ribbons. Add the greens to the onion and cook on medium heat for 10 minutes until wilted. Add garlic and cook 1 more minute. Then add streak o' lean and broth. Bring to a boil, reduce heat, and allow to simmer, partially covered, for 1 hour.

You can dress up collards by serving them with homemade chowchow, fresh diced tomatoes, onions, and cornbread.

POTLIKKER

Pot liquor, or potlikker as we call it in the South, is the flavorful broth left over from braising tough greens, like collards. Crumble cornbread in leftover potlikker and you've got a delicious, Southern treat full of nutrients like vitamin A and C. You can also pour it over your black-eyed peas and serve with cornbread

BLACK-EYED PEA SALAD WITH HOT BACON DRESSING

The luck traditions continue with black-eyed peas signifying wealth and prosperity. My papa always encouraged me to eat my peas if I wanted to be rich with coins. And if you found the penny cooked in the pot of peas, you would be especially lucky in the coming year. As much as I love the tradition of ringing in the New Year with them, they can be bland if not handled correctly. That's why I like to spice mine up with some unexpected heat and sweetness. My family can't get enough of this Hot Bacon Dressing; the perfect way to elevate a classic holiday dish. This dish is also a great leftover.

BLACK-EYED PEA SALAD	HOT BACON DRESSING
3 cups frozen black-eyed peas	5 slices bacon
5 green onions, sliced	1/4 cup cider vinegar
1/2 red bell pepper, chopped	2 tablespoons olive oil
1/2 green bell pepper, chopped	1 tablespoon granulated sugar
1/2 cup chopped red onion	1 teaspoon grated shallot
Salt and pepper, to taste	1/8 teaspoon dry mustard
Fresh parsley, chopped	2 tablespoons water

Prepare peas according to package directions, simmering only until al dente; drain and let cool. Place peas in a serving dish and add green onions, bell peppers, and red onion. Pour Hot Bacon Dressing over vegetables and toss to coat. Season with salt and pepper and garnish with parsley.

HOT BACON DRESSING

In a large skillet over medium heat, cook bacon until crisp. Remove bacon from skillet and drain on paper towels. Cut bacon into small pieces. Drain all but 2 tablespoons of bacon grease from the skillet. Add the remaining ingredients and cook over medium-high heat just until the liquid comes to a boil. Remove from heat. Add the bacon and whisk ingredients together. Serve hot over Black-Eyed Pea Salad.

SKILLET CORNBREAD

SERVES 8

In the South, a well-seasoned cast iron skillet is worth its weight in gold. Making cornbread in a well-seasoned cast iron skillet enhances flavor and gives cornbread an irresistible crunchy crust. When my great-grandmother Lorene Carpenter passed, the only thing my mother asked for was her cast iron skillet.

Papa, my maternal grandfather, used to eat cornbread crumbled up in buttermilk every night before bed. He considered it his dessert! In fact, I don't remember a meal ever eaten at my grandparents' house when warm cornbread and softened butter weren't served.

I cup plus I tablespoon plain fresh-ground cornmeal, divided

1/2 teaspoon salt

1/4 teaspoon baking soda

I heaping teaspoon baking powder

3/4 cup buttermilk

1/4 cup canola oil

1/2 cup water

2 tablespoons bacon grease

Preheat oven to 475 degrees.

Combine 1 cup cornmeal, salt, baking soda, baking powder, buttermilk, oil, and water in a bowl and mix well.

Add bacon grease to a 10-inch cast iron skillet and place in the oven for 5 minutes to melt. This will give the cornbread a crunchy crust and add flavor. Remove from oven and sprinkle 1 tablespoon of corn meal into the skillet before pouring in the cornbread mixture. The batter should sizzle when it hits the hot skillet. Bake for 25 minutes.

Tip: Freshly milled cornmeal makes all the difference in the texture of cornbread. You must store it in the refrigerator or freezer to keep it's freshness as there are no preservatives. If you can't find a source for freshly milled, store-bought stone-ground coarse-grind will do.

LEMON CHESS PIE

This pie seems like an unconventional choice for January, but I love the bright, tangy flavor after a long season of traditional holiday pies. Consider it a bright refreshing start to a new year full of fresh ideas and adventures!

1 recipe SB Pie Dough (page 17)

8 tablespoons (1 stick) unsalted butter

1 cup granulated sugar

3 egg yolks

3 tablespoons all-purpose flour

3 tablespoons cornmeal

2 1/2 tablespoons lemon zest

2 tablespoons lemon juice

3/4 cup buttermilk

1/2 teaspoon vanilla

Preheat oven to 350 degrees.

Roll out dough into a 12-inch circle. Place into a 9-inch round pie plate and flute.

In the mixing bowl of a stand mixer, cream together the butter and sugar. Add the yolks one at a time, beating after each addition. Add the flour and cornmeal slowly, beating until mixture is well-combined. Beat in the zest, juice, buttermilk, and vanilla. The mixture will appear lightly curdled. Pour into the pie shell. Bake in lower third of oven for 40–50 minutes. You will know the pie is done when the edges are set and there is a slight jiggle just in the center of the pie.

Remove from oven and let cool before serving. Store in the refrigerator.

FEBRUARY
Romantic Valentine's Repast

....

Valentine's Day is one of my favorite holidays. With the emergence of technology, it is rare that we find moments to simply gather and connect with one another without distractions. With all the craziness in our daily lives, I love taking the opportunity to escape the noise to create an elegant meal for my husband and me to share. That's why the recipes in this chapter are specifically designed to be as simple as they are delicious—so that you can spend less time in the kitchen, and more time connecting with the person (or people) you love.

....

Bacon-Wrapped Filets

Roasted Green Beans

Roma Tomato Tart

Parmesan-Herb Pie Crackers

Scalloped Potatoes

Strawberries and Cream Pie Pops

BACON-WRAPPED FILETS

SERVES 4

Everything about these filets is great. From their decadent, smoky bacon crust, to the juicy, sizzling meat, they are the perfect date-night food. They are also quick and easy to prepare while making the kitchen smell absolutely out-of-this-world.

4 (6-ounce) Prime beef filets
4 slices bacon
12 toothpicks
1 teaspoon kosher salt
1 teaspoon black pepper
1/2 teaspoon garlic powder
2 tablespoons butter
1 tablespoon olive oil
4 sprigs fresh thyme

Preheat oven to 500 degrees.

Pat filets dry with a paper towel. Wrap each with 1 slice of bacon, using toothpicks to hold bacon in place. Season both sides of filets with salt, pepper, and garlic powder.

Heat butter and oil in a large cast iron skillet over medium-high heat. Place steaks in skillet and sear for 2 minutes on each side. Remove skillet from stovetop and place in oven for 8 minutes.

Remove skillet from oven and quickly spoon pan juices over filets to baste. Check internal temperature of filets. Medium rare should read 130 degrees. If further cooking is desired, place skillet back in oven for an additional 2 minutes. Remove and let steaks rest on a plate for 3–5 minutes before serving. Garnish each steak with thyme.

ROASTED GREEN BEANS

SERVES 6

This simple side dish is as versatile as it is beautiful, adding just the right touch of color and robust flavor to any plate.

2 pounds green beans, trimmed

2 tablespoons olive oil

2 teaspoons kosher salt

I teaspoon freshly ground black pepper

1/4 teaspoon garlic powder

Crushed red pepper flakes, to taste, optional

Shaved Parmesan cheese, to taste, optional

Preheat oven to 400 degrees. Line a baking sheet with parchment paper.

Place beans in a shallow bowl and add the oil, salt, pepper, and garlic powder; toss to evenly coat.

Arrange green beans on baking sheet in a single layer. Bake for 15 minutes, or until beans are tender. For additional flavor add crushed red pepper flakes or shaved Parmesan.

ROMA TOMATO TART

Packed with rich, earthy flavors like fontina cheese and fresh tomatoes, this easy-to-make tart pairs beautifully with roasted meats.

> 1 recipe SB Pie Dough (page 17)
> 1 garlic bulb
> 1/2 teaspoon olive oil
> 1 1/2 cups grated fontina cheese
> 6 Roma tomatoes, sliced

Roll out dough into a 12-inch circle and place into a 10 1/4-inch tart pan. Partially bake the dough (see page 20).

Preheat oven to 425 degrees.

Chop off the pointed end of the garlic bulb, drizzle with oil, and wrap in aluminum foil. Bake for 30 minutes. Remove from oven and set aside to cool. Reduce oven temperature to 350 degrees.

Once cooled, squeeze the garlic cloves evenly over the bottom of the pie crust. Sprinkle 1/2 cup cheese over the garlic. Arrange the tomato slices over the cheese and then sprinkle with remaining cheese. Bake for 30–35 minutes.

Note: If you are baking this in the summer, you can substitute garden-fresh tomatoes for the Roma tomatoes.

PARMESAN-HERB PIE CRACKERS

SERVES 10 TO 12

These are some of my favorite things to whip up in the kitchen. Not only are they easy and full of herby flavor, their lacy texture makes them an elegant, simple appetizer to serve alone or alongside your favorite dip.

2 recipes SB Pie Dough (page 17)

2 cups grated Parmesan cheese

1 tablespoon chopped fresh thyme

1 tablespoon chopped fresh rosemary

1 teaspoon freshly ground black pepper

1/4 cup unsalted butter, melted

Preheat oven to 375 degrees. Line 2 baking sheets with parchment paper.

Roll out dough into 2 (10-inch) squares. Place each square on a baking sheet.

Combine Parmesan, thyme, rosemary, and pepper in a bowl and mix together. Brush butter evenly over dough and sprinkle with Parmesan-herb mixture. Lightly press the mixture into the dough. Cut dough into small squares with a pastry wheel. Bake 10–15 minutes until golden. Break apart the crackers and serve.

SCALLOPED POTATOES

I learned to make scalloped potatoes from my husband Alex. My family asks him to make this side every time we grill steaks. There is just something so comforting about this creamy, rich dish. I can promise there will be no leftovers. You will literally want to scrape the bottom of the pan for the last crunchy, buttery bite.

8 tablespoons (1 stick) butter, plus extra

5 large russet potatoes, peeled and sliced thinly

4 teaspoons all-purpose flour, divided

Kosher salt, to taste

Freshly ground black pepper, to taste

1/2 cup diced onions

1 pint heavy cream

Preheat oven to 375 degrees.

Rub a 9 x 12-inch baking dish with butter. Cut the stick of butter into small cubes. Arrange a single layer of potatoes on the bottom of the dish, dust with 1 teaspoon of flour and sprinkle with salt and pepper. Dot potatoes with a few cubes of butter and sprinkle some of the onions over top. Repeat these steps 3 more times and then pour the cream over the potatoes. Bake, uncovered, in bottom third of oven for 45 minutes, or until bubbly and lightly browned.

STRAWBERRIES AND CREAM PIE POPS

MAKES 8 POPS

Strawberries and cream . . . is anything more romantic? Every year we make heart-shaped cherry hand pies at the bakery to celebrate Valentine's Day—but this version substitutes strawberries and adds a sweet sugary glaze, which make them even better! Although these are fun to make yourself, they also can be a fun holiday project for the kids to enjoy with you.

1 quart fresh strawberries, hulled and diced

1/4 cup granulated sugar

2 tablespoons all-purpose flour

2 recipes SB Pie Dough (page 17)

8 Popsicle sticks or cute paper straws

3 tablespoons heavy cream

4 tablespoons powdered sugar

8 teaspoons milk

Whipped cream

Preheat oven to 400 degrees. Line a baking sheet with parchment paper.

In a bowl, combine strawberries, granulated sugar, and flour. A sticky, sugary paste should begin to form in the bowl.

Roll out dough into 2 (12-inch) circles. Using a small knife or heart-shaped cookie cutter, cut 8 small hearts out of each circle of dough for a total of 16. Place 8 of the hearts on the baking sheet. Spoon the strawberry mix evenly into the center of each heart. Place 1 Popsicle stick into the filling of each heart. Brush edges of hearts with cream. Place remaining 8 hearts over the fruit and press around the edges to seal then brush each heart with cream.

Bake for 15 minutes, or until golden brown. Remove from baking sheet and place on a cooling rack.

Mix powdered sugar and milk together in a small bowl until smooth. Drizzle over each heart pop and let set for 45 minutes. Serve with whipped cream as a dipping sauce.

MARCH
Birthday Supper

March is such a beautiful month here in Georgia. Not only is it when we get the first hints of warm weather; it's also when the flowers start to bloom, and when my husband Alex celebrates his birthday. When we have a birthday in the family, I always like to plan a meal and make it at home. We avoid the chaos and confusion of a restaurant, and I get the chance to personalize the meal for whomever I'm celebrating. That's why all of the recipes in this chapter are Alex's personal favorites.

Zucchini Tart

Lemony Green Peas

Chicken Tarragon With Brown Rice

Cherry Pie Tassies

Boston Cream Pie

ZUCCHINI TART

I always enjoy making savory tarts to serve as appetizers at parties. This tart is sublime—savory, but also a little sweet because of the Vidalia onions.

1 recipe SB Pie Dough (page 17)

4 cups spiralized zucchini

4 tablespoons butter

1 cup chopped Vidalia onion

1/4 cup chopped fresh parsley

1 teaspoon salt

1 teaspoon freshly ground black pepper

2 eggs

2 teaspoons Dijon mustard

Roll out dough to a 14 1/2 x 5-inch rectangle and place in a 13 3/4 x 14 1/2-inch tart pan; prebake the dough (see page 20).

Preheat oven to 375 degrees.

Squeeze out any excess water from the zucchini. Set aside.

Place butter in a large skillet over medium-high heat and melt. Add onion and sauté for 5 minutes. Add zucchini, parsley, salt, and pepper, and sauté for an additional 3–4 minutes. Zucchini should be al dente but not taste raw. Remove from heat.

Whisk eggs in a bowl and gradually add to the skillet, stirring constantly to combine. Paint bottom of pie crust with mustard. Spoon zucchini mixture into tart shell and bake for 25–30 minutes.

LEMONY GREEN PEAS

SERVES 6

*There's nothing like taking a simple green vegetable and jazzing it up with citrusy flavors.
These easy-to-make peas brighten up any ordinary dinner!*

1 1/2 tablespoons olive oil

1 tablespoon butter

1 cup chopped Vidalia onion

2 cloves garlic, sliced

3 cups fresh or frozen and thawed green peas

1/2 teaspoon kosher salt

1/2 teaspoon freshly ground black pepper

1/2 teaspoon lemon zest

1 tablespoon fresh squeezed lemon juice

1 tablespoon chopped fresh mint leaves

Heat oil and butter in a skillet over medium-high heat. Add onion and sauté for 5 minutes. Add garlic and sauté for 1–2 more minutes. Add peas and sauté 5 minutes until peas are cooked though. Reduce heat. Add salt, pepper, zest, and juice and toss until combined. Remove from heat and garnish with mint. Serve warm.

CHICKEN TARRAGON
WITH BROWN RICE

SERVES 6

....

The first meal Alex cooked for me was chicken tarragon. The creamy, rich sauce combined with the slightly bittersweet flavor of the tarragon makes for a dish straight out of heaven!

1/4 cup butter

6 boneless, skinless chicken
   breasts, pounded to tenderize

Salt, to taste

Freshly ground black pepper,
   to taste

1/2 cup beef broth

1/2 cup Madeira

1 cup heavy cream

1 cup sliced mushrooms, sautéed
   in butter

1/2 teaspoon dried tarragon

Brown Rice

Preheat oven to 400 degrees. Melt butter in 12-inch skillet over medium heat. Season chicken with salt and pepper, add to skillet, and brown 3–4 minutes on each side. Remove to a shallow ovenproof plate and place in oven for 10 minutes. Add broth and Madeira to the skillet and cook until reduced by half. Add cream and bring to a rolling boil while stirring. Add chicken, drippings, mushrooms, and tarragon, and simmer until sauce has thickened, about 10 minutes. Serve over rice.

Brown Rice

SERVES 4

....

My favorite thing to eat as a child was rice smothered in homemade gravy.

1 tablespoon butter

1 cup brown rice

2 cups chicken broth

Melt butter in saucepan over medium heat. Add rice and cook for 2 minutes, stirring often. Add broth and bring to a boil. Reduce heat to low, cover, and cook for 50 minutes, or until rice is tender.

CHERRY PIE TASSIES

MAKES 24 TASSIES

Gone are the days of serving cake and cupcakes for birthdays. Step outside of your comfort zone and try this fun bite-size dessert. The balance of the sour cherries and sweet, sugary glaze is sure to delight!

2 recipes SB Pie Dough (page 17)
4 cups fresh or frozen and thawed sour cherries, pitted
1 cup granulated sugar
1/4 cup cornstarch
1/2 cup powdered sugar
1 cup heavy cream
1/2 teaspoon vanilla

Preheat oven to 375 degrees. Grease 1 (24-cup) mini-muffin pan.

Roll out dough into 2 (12-inch) circles. Cut 24 (3-inch) circles with a biscuit cutter. Press the dough circles into each muffin cup and place in the freezer for 20 minutes.

Combine cherries, sugar, and cornstarch in a bowl and mix until well-combined. Remove muffin pan from freezer and fill with cherry filling. Bake for 30 minutes, or until crust is golden brown. Remove from oven and set aside to cool.

Combine the powdered sugar, cream, and vanilla in a saucepan over medium heat and bring just to a simmer. Remove from heat. Once tassies are cooled, remove from pan and drizzle icing over top. Serve immediately.

BOSTON CREAM PIE

SERVES 8

Boston Cream Pie is one of Alex's favorite sweet treats. I can't say I blame him. It's hard not to think of the dessert without thinking of its elegant chocolate ganache topping or creamy custard filling. And the cake filling means you can have your cake and eat your pie too!

CAKE

1 recipe SB Pie Dough
   (page 17)

3 egg yolks, lightly beaten

1/2 cup milk, divided

1 1/2 teaspoons vanilla

3/4 cups granulated sugar

3 1/2 cups cake flour, sifted

1/2 tablespoon plus 1/2 teaspoon
   baking powder

Pinch of salt

6 tablespoons butter, softened

CUSTARD

1/3 cup granulated sugar

2 tablespoons cornstarch

1/8 teaspoon salt

1 cup milk

1 egg plus 1 egg yolk, well-beaten

1 tablespoon butter

1 teaspoon vanilla

GANACHE

2 tablespoons butter, melted

3/4 cup heavy cream

Pinch of salt

1 cup semisweet chocolate chips

CAKE

Preheat oven to 350 degrees.

Roll out dough into a 12-inch circle. Place into a 9-inch round pie plate and flute.

In a small bowl, combine egg yolks, 1/4 cup milk, and vanilla.

In a mixer fitted with the paddle attachment, mix together the sugar, flour, baking powder, and salt on low for 1 minute. Mix in butter and remaining milk. Once all the ingredients are incorporated, mix on medium speed and beat for 90 seconds. Add the egg mixture in batches, beating for 20 seconds after each addition. Pour into pie crust.

Bake for 25 minutes, or until a toothpick inserted into the center comes out clean. Place on rack to cool.

CUSTARD

In a 1-quart glass bowl, blend together the sugar, cornstarch, and salt. Gradually stir in milk, mixing well. Microwave on high 5–7 minutes, stirring every 3 minutes until mixture is smooth, thickened, and clear.

Stir a small amount of hot pudding quickly into the eggs. Return egg mixture to hot pudding, mixing well. Microwave at medium-high for 1–3 minutes, stirring after 1 minute until smooth and thickened. Add butter and vanilla, stirring until butter is melted into custard. Let cool and then refrigerate until ready to assemble pie.

GANACHE

In a small saucepan, heat butter, cream, and salt until it just comes to a simmer. Pour the hot cream mixture over the chocolate chips. Whisk until ganache is smooth and shiny.

When the cake is cooled and the custard is cold, spread the custard over the cake. Then pour the warm ganache on top of the custard. Smooth with a spatula.

APRIL
Easter Brunch

Easter is one of our most beautiful holidays here in Georgia. Growing up, we always spent Easters with Grandmother Betty and Granddaddy. We'd wake up before dawn to attend the sunrise service at church where Granddaddy led the choir and Betty accompanied on the organ. As the service ended, we would disperse and reconvene at my grandparents' house for a delicious Easter breakfast, followed by an Easter egg hunt.

These recipes are perfect for a post-church brunch as you catch up with loved ones, hide Easter eggs for the kids, and celebrate the resurrection this season represents!

Apple, Pear, and Sausage Breakfast Pie

Braided Ham and Swiss Pastry

Celery, Date, and Pecan Butter Pie Bites

Melon and Strawberry Arugula Salad

Apricot Pie in Mason Jar Lids

Easter Pie Cookies with Royal Icing

APPLE, PEAR, AND SAUSAGE BREAKFAST PIE

SERVES 8

. . . .

This recipe is inspired by my mother-in-law Sandy Wilbanks. The unexpected mix of sweet, juicy fruit with savory sausage is the perfect combination of hearty winter flavors and light, summery ones, too.

1 recipe SB Pie Dough (page 17)
2 pears, cored and chopped
3 Granny Smith apples, cored and chopped
1 cup apple cider
1/4 cup brown sugar
1/8 teaspoon ground cinnamon
1/8 teaspoon ground cloves
1/8 teaspoon thyme
1/4 teaspoon kosher salt
Pinch of ground nutmeg
1 pound sausage (I use Stripling's Sage Sausage), cooked and drained
1 cup grated sharp cheddar cheese

Roll out dough into a 12-inch circle. Place into a 9-inch pie plate and flute; partially bake the dough (see page 20).

Preheat oven to 375 degrees.

Combine the pears, apples, cider, brown sugar, cinnamon, cloves, thyme and salt in a bowl. Place mixture in a large skillet and sauté over medium-low heat until the apples are tender enough to pierce with a fork. Remove from heat. Using a slotted spoon, transfer the apples and pears to a bowl and set aside. There should be about 1 cup of liquid left in the skillet. Cook the liquid on medium heat until reduced by half, about 10 minutes.

Combine the sausage with the apples and pears. Add the reduced liquid and stir to combine. Pour into pie crust and sprinkle cheese evenly over top. Bake for 40 minutes.

BRAIDED HAM AND SWISS PASTRY

This dish is inspired by my mom's ham, Swiss, and Dijon petite sandwiches. Every time my mom hosted a shower, which was often in the South, as we shower everyone for everything, she would make these sandwiches. It was all I could do to refrain from eating almost all of them. This is my version of a classic favorite with a beautiful new twist. It looks every bit as elegant and sophisticated at a baby or wedding shower as it does at Easter brunch. Yet, it's so beautiful no one will realize it only took a few minutes to assemble!

4 tablespoons (1/2 stick) unsalted butter, melted

2 ounces cream cheese, softened

1 cup finely chopped Vidalia onion

3 tablespoons Dijon mustard

1 1/2 teaspoons poppy seeds

1 1/2 teaspoons sesame seeds

1 teaspoon Worcestershire sauce

1/2 pound grated Swiss cheese

1 recipe SB Pie Dough (page 17)

1/2 pound baked ham, shredded

1/4 cup heavy cream

1/4 teaspoon kosher salt

1/4 teaspoon freshly cracked black pepper

Preheat oven to 400 degrees. Place a wire rack inside a half sheet pan.

Combine the butter, cream cheese, onion, mustard, poppy seeds, sesame seeds, Worcestershire sauce, and Swiss cheese in a bowl.

Roll out dough to a 12-inch circle. Place dough on a piece of parchment paper cut to the same size as the sheet pan. Leaving a 4-inch-wide space down the center of the dough for the filling, cut even strips on both sides, from the center out. Arrange the ham in the center of the dough and spoon cheese mixture on top of ham. Crisscross the strips over the filling. Brush the top of the pastry with cream and sprinkle with salt and pepper. Slide parchment with pastry onto the wire rack. Bake, uncovered, for 15 minutes then reduce heat to 325 degrees and bake for 30–35 minutes, or until golden brown. Slice and serve immediately.

CELERY, DATE, AND PECAN BUTTER PIE BITES

MAKES 8 PIE BITES

At Southern Baked Pie Company, we get our pecans from South Georgia Pecan Company; so I wanted to incorporate their amazing pecan butter into a recipe for this book. These beautiful appetizers are positively packed with buttery pecan flavor and a touch of sweetness.

I recipe SB Pie Dough (page 17)

I egg white, beaten

I Fuji apple, chopped

2 stalks celery, chopped

3 dates, chopped

I 1/2 cups Purely Pecans Pecan Butter—Sea Salt Y'all
(substitute with almond butter)

Honey, to taste

Preheat oven to 375 degrees. Line a baking sheet with parchment paper.

Roll out dough into a 10-inch square. Cut 4 (3 x 3-inch) squares out of the dough. Cut each square in half to make triangles. Place the triangles of dough on baking sheet. Using a fork, prick each triangle. Brush with the egg white. Bake for 15 minutes. Remove from oven and let cool on baking rack.

In a small bowl, combine the apple, celery, and dates.

To serve, place a dollop of pecan butter on each triangle, sprinkle with apple mixture, and then drizzle with honey.

MELON AND STRAWBERRY ARUGULA SALAD

SERVES 8 TO 10

This salad is light and fresh—perfect for pairing with some of the heavier items on the table. The bite of the arugula mixed with the sweetness of the melon is a complex, enchanting flavor combination that'll have even the pickiest eaters coming back for seconds.

4 tablespoons olive oil

1 tablespoon freshly squeezed lemon juice

1 tablespoon honey

2 tablespoons chopped fresh mint

2 tablespoons chopped fresh parsley

2 tablespoons chopped fresh chives

2 cups melon balls, cantaloupe or honeydew

2 cups fresh strawberries, halved

3 cups baby arugula

In a small bowl, whisk together the oil, lemon juice, honey, mint, parsley, and chives to make a dressing.

In a large bowl, combine the melon balls and strawberries. Add the dressing and toss to coat. Arrange the arugula on a serving platter and top with the melon mixture.

APRICOT PIE IN MASON JAR LIDS

Making little pies in Mason jar lids takes me back to my childhood. My mother and grandmother canned everything—from freshly strung green beans to homemade tomato soups and jellies. The one thing that always bothered me was that we had to wait to eat the freshly canned foods. So, I created this recipe in honor of them. I don't have to wait to eat these little pies. They are best served warm, right out of the oven.

> 2 recipes SB Pie Dough (page 17)
> 6 Mason jar lids
> 1 cup apricot preserves
> 1/2 cup cream cheese, softened
> 1/4 cup heavy cream
> 1/2 cup granulated sugar

Preheat oven to 375 degrees. Line a baking sheet with parchment paper.

Roll out dough into 2 (12-inch) circles. Cut 12 circles out of each dough round, slightly larger than the Mason jar lids. You should have a total of 24 circles. Press circles of dough into the bottom and up the sides of 12 jar lids.

Spoon 1 heaping tablespoon of apricot preserves into each shell. Top with 2 teaspoons of softened cream cheese. Place remaining dough circles on top of the filling. Press to seal. Brush with heavy cream and sprinkle with sugar.

Place on baking sheet. Bake for 15 minutes, and then reduce heat to 325 degrees and continue to bake for 20 minutes. Remove from oven and pop each pie out of their lid and let cool on a wire rack.

EASTER PIE COOKIES
WITH ROYAL ICING

MAKES 2 DOZEN COOKIES

Did you know Southern Baked Pie Dough is amazing in the form of a cookie? The flaky texture combined with the slightly sweet and saltiness yields a kid- and adult-friendly treat. I love to gather the kids in the kitchen for a little cookie making time on Easter weekend. As we work together cutting out shapes in the dough, this gives me the opportunity to explain the true meaning of Easter.

> 2 recipes SB Pie Dough (page 17)
> 2 egg whites
> 1 (1-pound) box powdered sugar
> 1 to 2 tablespoons water

Preheat oven to 400 degrees. Line a baking sheet with parchment paper.

Roll out dough into 2 (12-inch) circles. Cut out desired shapes with Easter cookie cutters. Place cookies on baking sheet. Prick each cookie with the tines of a fork, and bake for 15 minutes, or until golden brown.

Using a stand mixer, beat egg whites with whisk attachment until frothy. Reduce speed and gradually add in the sugar. Once well-combined, turn mixer up to high and beat until stiff peaks form. Add food coloring to icing if desired.

Place icing in piping bags and decorate cookies, allowing 1 hour for icing to set up.

MAY
Mother's Day Lunch

My mother and grandmothers have such a special place in my heart, not least because they taught me how to cook. My mother taught me how to throw a delicious weeknight meal together in thirty minutes flat. She could hold a toddler, fluff a load of laundry, make biscuits from scratch, and stir the homemade gravy so that it didn't scorch, all while calling out sight words to me from across the kitchen counter. Southern women can multitask like no other.

Later, it was my mother-in-law Sandy who taught me how to bake homemade pie. That's why Mother's Day is such a special time in my family. I love gathering the mothers and mother figures in my life so that I can celebrate them for all the wonderful things they do. These recipes were especially created for a Mother's Day lunch, to be elegant, easy, and delicious.

Chicken Salad Timbales

Paradise Soup

Roasted Carrots with Vinaigrette Dressing

Mock Champagne

Spinach and Mushroom Quiche

Three Berry Slab Pie with Granola Topping

CHICKEN SALAD TIMBALES

SERVES 8

Nothing says "Southern hospitality" to me quite like chicken salad. I always like to have some on hand at home in case guests swing by—that and a pitcher of sweet tea are the perfect and quick welcome foods. These timbales are just the Southern appetizer your lunch needs to get started off on the right foot. Pour a glass of sweet tea and enjoy!

2 recipes SB Pie Dough (page 17)
1 whole roasted chicken
1/2 cup chopped celery
1 cup green grapes, halved
1 cup red grapes, halved
1 1/2 cups mayonnaise (I use Dukes)
1 cup chopped toasted pecans
Kosher salt, to taste
Freshly ground black pepper, to taste
Fresh mint leaves
Pecan oil

Preheat oven to 375 degrees.

Roll out dough into 2 (12-inch) circles. Cut circles just big enough to fill 8 (4-inch) tart pans. Line the tart pans with dough; prebake tart shells (see page 20). Set aside to cool.

Remove the meat from the chicken, shred, and place in a large bowl with the celery, grapes, mayonnaise, and pecans; gently mix to combine. Season with salt and pepper.

Spoon the chicken salad into the tart shells, garnish with mint, and lightly drizzle with oil before serving.

PARADISE SOUP

SERVES 8

My mother-in-law loves to make and serve this bright, refreshing soup. One taste will show you why! It is simple to make, yet bursting with flavor. It can also be made ahead and frozen; so it's great for celebrations where there's a lot going on.

2 large, ripe tomatoes

1 clove garlic, crushed

2 teaspoons granulated sugar

1/2 teaspoon kosher salt

1 teaspoon freshly ground black pepper

8 cups tomato juice, plus extra

2 cups sour cream, plus extra

3 large unpeeled cucumbers

1 cup chopped fresh parsley

Bring a large saucepan of water to a boil; plunge tomatoes into boiling water for 30 seconds. Remove quickly and transfer to an ice bath to stop the cooking. Peel off skins and cut into quarters. To purée, press tomatoes through a fine mesh sieve into a large bowl; add the garlic, sugar, salt, pepper, and 8 cups of tomato juice. Refrigerate to chill.

When ready to serve, taste and adjust seasoning if needed. If soup is too thick add additional tomato juice; stir in sour cream.

Cut each cucumber into 8 spears. Serve chilled soup in individual cups with cucumbers, a dollop of sour cream, and parsley, to garnish. Or you can dress up this soup and serve it in bowls with chopped cucumber sprinkled in the sour cream.

ROASTED CARROTS WITH VINAIGRETTE DRESSING

SERVES 6

One of my all-time favorite recipes—the sweetness of the roasted carrots combined with the herby vinaigrette will take your taste buds on the most pleasing journey!

2 pounds baby carrots

3/4 cup olive oil, divided

2 tablespoons kosher salt

2 tablespoons freshly ground black pepper

4 tablespoons white wine vinegar

2 tablespoons whole grain mustard

2 tablespoons minced garlic

7 fresh thyme sprigs, minced

3 sprigs fresh rosemary, minced

Preheat oven to 475 degrees. Line a large baking sheet with parchment paper.

In a large bowl, toss the carrots with 4 tablespoons oil, salt, and pepper. Arrange carrots in single layer on baking sheet. Bake for 20 minutes or until fork tender. Turn carrots halfway through the baking time.

In a small bowl, whisk together the vinegar, mustard, garlic, thyme, rosemary, and remaining oil.

Pour the vinaigrette over the warm carrots to serve.

MOCK CHAMPAGNE

When ladies gather together in the South, there is always a punch cocktail, or mocktail served along with sweet iced tea.

3/4 cup granulated sugar

1 cup water

1 cup canned grapefruit juice

1/2 cup fresh pineapple juice

1 quart ginger ale

Fresh mint leaves, optional

Fresh strawberries, optional

Pineapple chunks, optional

Mix sugar and water in a saucepan. Bring to boil and cook 5 minutes; remove from heat and set aside to cool. Add fruit juices to sugar syrup; chill. Add ginger ale before serving. Garnish with mint, strawberries, and pineapple chunks, if desired.

SPINACH AND MUSHROOM QUICHE

SERVES 8 PER QUICHE

This staple is the most popular quiche served in any of our Southern Baked pie shops, and I'll let you in on a little secret—it's incredibly easy to make at home! Chock-full of spinach and mushrooms, this quiche is not overly eggy. The recipe makes two quiches. Bake both, enjoy one, and freeze the other for easy reheating.

2 recipes SB Pie Dough (page 17)

6 tablespoons butter

1 cup chopped Vidalia onion

1 pound sliced mushrooms

3 eggs

1 cup full-fat plain Greek yogurt

1/8 teaspoon ground nutmeg

3/4 teaspoon kosher salt

1/2 teaspoon freshly ground pepper

1 (10-ounce) package frozen chopped spinach, thawed and drained

12 ounces grated Gruyère cheese

Roll out dough into 2 (12-inch) circles. Place into 2 (9-inch) round pie plates and flute; prebake the dough (see page 20).

Preheat oven to 375 degrees.

Melt butter in a large skillet over medium-high heat. Add onion and sauté, about 5 minutes. Add mushrooms and cook, stirring frequently, until mushrooms are golden and liquid has evaporated, 8–10 minutes. Transfer to a bowl and let cool.

In a medium bowl, whisk together eggs and yogurt until combined. Add nutmeg, salt, and pepper. Add the spinach and mushroom mixture; stir to combine.

Cover the bottom of each crust with 1/4 of the cheese. Divide filling in half and pour over cheese. Top each quiche with remaining cheese. Bake until set in the center, 25–30 minutes. Serve warm or at room temperature.

THREE BERRY SLAB PIE WITH GRANOLA TOPPING

SERVES 8

When I was young I used to pick blueberries at my grandparents' house, partially because those berries would often make their way into a slab pie or cobbler later in the afternoon. Slab pies are a great way to make pie for a crowd. Just cut into squares, serve with vanilla ice cream, and get ready to smile.

2 recipes SB Pie Dough
  (page 17)
1 1/2 cups raspberries
2 cups blackberries
2 cups blueberries
1/4 cup granulated sugar
2 tablespoons cornstarch
1 teaspoon fresh lemon juice
1 1/2 cups slivered almonds
3 cups rolled oats
1 cup unsweetened coconut

1 cup pumpkin seeds
1 cup sunflower seeds
1/2 teaspoon ground nutmeg
1 teaspoon coarse salt
1 teaspoon vanilla
1 teaspoon ground cinnamon
1/2 cup maple syrup
1/4 cup honey
1/3 cup canola oil
1/4 cup butter, cubed

Butter an 8 x 8-inch glass baking dish. Roll out dough into a 12-inch square. Line the bottom and sides of the baking dish with the dough; partially bake dough (see page 20).

Preheat oven to 375 degrees.

In a large bowl, combine the berries, sugar, cornstarch, and lemon juice. Pour mixture into the crust.

In a large bowl, mix together the almonds, oats, coconut, pumpkin seeds, sunflower seeds, nutmeg, salt, vanilla, cinnamon, syrup, honey, and oil. Sprinkle evenly over berry filling. Dot with cubes of butter.

Bake in bottom third of oven for 30 minutes. Cover with aluminum foil and bake an additional 30 minutes until bubbly. Serve warm with vanilla ice cream.

JUNE
Father's Day Party

I have a lot of things in common with my dad; but the thing I appreciate and love most is the entrepreneurial spirit we share. Growing up, it was my father who taught me about the importance of hard work and dedication—skills which helped me when I first opened Southern Baked Pie Company years ago. His encouragement and tenacity gave me the strength to continue even on the busiest, most difficult days.

For me, Father's Day is a unique, fun chance to celebrate the men who have meant the most to me—first my dad and now my husband, Alex, who has been such a wonderful father to our two boys. That's why the recipes in this chapter are handpicked to be outdoor barbeque and he-man friendly. Each one is a crowd-pleaser, perfect for making ahead and throwing on the grill, or in the bowl, while you enjoy the company of loved ones, especially the fathers or father figures in your life.

Smoked Boston Butt Sliders

Summer Coleslaw

Southern-Style BBQ Sauce

Roasted Potato Salad with Herb Dressing

Chocolate Bourbon Pecan Pie

Blackberry Hand Pies

SMOKED BOSTON BUTT SLIDERS

MAKES 24 MINI SLIDERS

....

These smoky, bite-size sliders are absolutely perfect for celebrating your favorite guys, not only because they're stuffed with the kind of tender, succulent meat guys dream about, but also because they're the ideal dish for a cookout. Smoke this roast on the grill while you enjoy the day outside with your family or, put dad himself in charge. Regardless of how you do it, these sweet, spicy, saucy treats will have everyone in a celebratory mood. Serve with slaw on top for an extra layer of cool, smooth flavor.

1/4 cup brown sugar
1 tablespoon kosher salt
1 tablespoon black pepper
1 tablespoon paprika
1/2 tablespoon cayenne pepper
1 (5-pound) Boston butt pork roast
1 (12-ounce) bottle dark beer
1/4 cup apple cider vinegar
24 mini slider buns
Southern-Style BBQ Sauce (page 100)
Summer Coleslaw (page 99)

Preheat smoker to 225 degrees.

Combine brown sugar, salt, pepper, paprika, and cayenne in a bowl. Rub the entire roast with spice mix and place in the smoker with fat cap on top. Smoke for 4 hours. Remove from smoker, place roast in a disposable foil roasting pan, and pour the beer and vinegar over top. Cover with aluminum foil and return to the smoker. Smoke for 3–4 more hours, until tender.

Remove roast from smoker and let rest at room temperature for 20 minutes before shredding. To serve, dress the slider buns with the sauce, add some meat, and top with a small scoop of coleslaw.

SUMMER COLESLAW

It's a well-known fact that no Southern barbeque celebration worth its salt would ever leave out the coleslaw. This summery recipe adds an extra-special southern twist with Vidalia onions and apple cider vinegar. My mother-in-law, Sandy, made this for Alex on his first Father's Day and it's been a favorite in our family ever since.

1/2 green cabbage, shredded

1 small Vidalia onion, thinly sliced

1 teaspoon salt

1/2 teaspoon freshly ground black pepper

2 tablespoons granulated sugar

1/2 teaspoon celery seeds

1/4 cup sour cream

1/2 cup mayonnaise

1 1/2 tablespoons apple cider vinegar

Toss the cabbage and onion together in a large mixing bowl. Sprinkle with salt, pepper, sugar, and celery seed; mix together.

Combine the sour cream, mayonnaise, and vinegar until blended well. Pour over the cabbage mixture and toss thoroughly.

SOUTHERN-STYLE BBQ SAUCE

MAKES 3/4 CUP

Sweet and tangy, this sauce has just the right amount of kick to make your taste buds dance!

1/2 cup mayonnaise
1/4 cup apple cider vinegar
1 tablespoon brown sugar
1 tablespoon Sriracha sauce
1/2 teaspoon salt

Combine all ingredients in a small bowl and whisk until smooth. Cover and refrigerate until ready for use. Keep stored in refrigerator for up to two weeks.

ROASTED POTATO SALAD WITH HERB DRESSING

As a daughter of the South, my love for Southern potato salad began at first bite, sitting around my grandmother and papa's farm table. My papa loved his "tater salad" as he called it. My grandmother made the BEST potato salad. She brought it to every family reunion, church picnic, or dinner on the grounds. This potato salad is bursting with the succulent flavor of fresh herbs. Roasting the potatoes cuts down on the cooking time, not to mention mess in the kitchen. The vibrantly flavored creamy dressing complements the potatoes perfectly, and pairs beautifully with sweet, salty barbecue.

3 pounds small red potatoes, washed and cubed

2 tablespoons olive oil

1 teaspoon kosher salt

1 teaspoon freshly ground black pepper

1 cup mayonnaise

1/2 cup sour cream

2 tablespoons chopped fresh parsley

1 tablespoon chopped fresh dill

1 tablespoon chopped fresh thyme

2 cloves garlic, minced

Preheat oven to 400 degrees. Line a large baking sheet with parchment paper.

Spread potatoes onto baking sheet, drizzle with oil, and sprinkle with salt and pepper. Roast for 25 minutes. Remove and let cool before transferring to a large bowl.

Whisk together the mayonnaise, sour cream, parsley, dill, thyme, and garlic in a small bowl. Pour over potatoes and toss to coat. Taste and adjust seasonings if necessary.

CHOCOLATE BOURBON PECAN PIE

SERVES 8

It's not hard to see why this boozy pecan pie is one of Alex's all-time favorites. Between its deep, rich flavor and very masculine look, it makes the perfect topper for a delicious Father's Day meal . . . or any meal at all, for that matter.

I recipe SB Pie Dough (page 17)

3 ounces bittersweet chocolate, chopped

3 large eggs, lightly beaten

1/2 cup packed brown sugar

3 tablespoons unsalted butter, melted

3/4 cup dark corn syrup

I teaspoon vanilla

3 tablespoons whiskey

1 1/2 cups whole pecans

Roll out dough into a 12-inch circle. Place into a 9-inch round pie plate and flute; prebake the dough (see page 20).

Preheat oven to 375 degrees.

Remove pie crust from oven and immediately sprinkle chocolate over bottom of crust. Let melt then spread with spatula to cover completely.

Mix together the eggs, brown sugar, butter, syrup, vanilla, and whiskey in a bowl until combined. Sprinkle pecans over chocolate and pour the filling over pecans. Bake for 40 minutes, or until filling is just set. Let cool before serving.

BLACKBERRY HAND PIES

MAKES 5 HAND PIES

Blackberry pies are a limited-edition item at Southern Baked Pie Company, and they're always a big hit. Nothing says "summer has arrived" quite like a fresh batch of blackberries. Their perfect balance of sweetness and tartness makes them a universal hit with kids and adults alike. To me, these hand pies taste like a grown-up toaster strudel. Plus, the kids or grandkids will love getting in the kitchen to help you make these delicious treats.

4 cups fresh blackberries

1 1/2 cups granulated sugar, divided

4 tablespoons cornstarch

1 egg

1 tablespoon water

2 recipes SB Pie Dough (page 17)

Preheat oven to 400 degrees. Line a baking sheet with parchment paper.

In a large bowl, mix together the blackberries, 1 cup sugar, and cornstarch.

Whisk together the egg and water in a small bowl to make an egg wash.

Roll out dough into 2 (12- inch) squares. Cut 5 (5^{1}/2 x 3^{1}/2-inch) rectangles out of each square. Reroll scraps of dough if needed to get all the rectangles. Spoon blackberry filling into the middle of 5 of the rectangles and brush the edges with egg wash. Top with remaining rectangles and seal edges with a fork.

Transfer hand pies to baking sheet. Brush the tops with remaining egg wash and sprinkle with remaining sugar. Bake for 25 minutes, or until golden brown. Serve warm.

JULY
Independence Day Celebration

The Fourth of July has been one of my favorite holidays ever since I was a little girl. In those halcyon days, my whole family would go up to our lake house on Lake Burton—parents, grandparents, aunts, uncles, and cousins. We spent the day cooking, eating, laughing, and just plain being together. Now, I get to take my own family to the place that is more than a lake house. It is a house of memories, where Alex and I now share those beloved traditions with our two sons every summer.

The recipes in this chapter are perfect for getting your whole family into the patriotic spirit, and for munching on throughout the day. Dishes like Fried Squash (page 117) will take you right back to memories of childhood summers, while fun, festive treats like the All-American Pie Shooters (page 118) will gather everyone together faster than a fireworks show on the shore.

Bourbon-Marinated Flank Steak

Tomato Corn Pie

Pimiento Cheese Pie Bites

Fried Squash

All-American Pie Shooters

BOURBON-MARINATED FLANK STEAK

SERVES 4

Flank steak is my go-to dish for parties by the lake because it serves a crowd and is easy to prepare. Marinate in my signature Asian-inspired, salty-sweet sauce the night before and throw on the grill for an effortless dish everyone will be sure to love.

1 1/2 pounds flank steak
1/4 cup brown sugar
1/4 cup bourbon
3 tablespoons soy sauce
1 tablespoon lime juice
2 teaspoons Worcestershire sauce
1/3 cup warm water
2 tablespoons grated fresh ginger
2 cloves garlic, minced
1/2 teaspoon freshly ground black pepper
1/8 teaspoon hot pepper sauce

Score flank steak and place in a gallon-size ziplock bag. Mix remaining ingredients together in a bowl and pour over flank steak. Seal the bag and turn to coat the steak. Marinate overnight in the refrigerator.

Grill until medium rare, or to your liking. Slice thinly across the grain to serve.

TOMATO CORN PIE

SERVES 8

Before we arrived at Lake Burton, my family would always stop at the local farmers market and pick up all the fresh fruits and vegetables we needed for the holiday weekend. In honor of that tradition, this delicious pie combines two of my absolute favorite summer vegetables—tomatoes and fresh corn. Cheesy, but full of garden veggies and bright flavors, this dish is the epitome of summer.

1 recipe SB pie dough (page 17)
2 large tomatoes, sliced
1 teaspoon kosher salt
1/3 cup mayonnaise
1/4 cup sour cream
2 tablespoons fresh lemon juice
2 tablespoons chopped fresh basil
2 teaspoons freshly ground black pepper
2 cups fresh corn kernels
2 cups grated mozzarella cheese

Preheat oven to 375 degrees.

Roll out dough into a 12-inch circle. Place into a 9-inch pie plate and flute the edges.

Place tomato slices on a paper towel and sprinkle with salt; set aside.

Whisk together the mayonnaise, sour cream, lemon juice, basil, and pepper in a small bowl.

Sprinkle bottom of pie crust with 1/4 cup cheese. Arrange half of the tomatoes over the cheese and sprinkle with corn. Cover with half of the mayonnaise mixture. Repeat layering with remaining tomatoes, corn, and mayonnaise mixture. Sprinkle remaining cheese over the top.

Bake for 1 hour, or until bubbly. Cover with aluminum foil if cheese begins to brown too quickly.

PIMIENTO CHEESE PIE BITES

MAKES 24 PIE BITES

Pimiento cheese is a Southern staple, and I always keep some in my fridge along with sweet tea and chicken salad in case guests stop by. These creamy pimiento cheese bites, with a kick of garlic and jalapeño, are the ideal warm-weather appetizer.

2 recipes SB Pie Dough (page 17)

3 cups grated extra sharp cheddar cheese

2 cups grated white cheddar cheese

1 1/2 cups mayonnaise (I use Duke's)

1 1/2 cups diced pimientos

1/4 cup seeds removed and diced jalapeño peppers

2 tablespoons finely chopped Vidalia onion

1 clove garlic, grated

1 cup chopped pecans

Preheat oven to 375 degrees. Grease a 24-cup mini-muffin pan.

Roll out dough into a 2 (12-inch) circles. Cut 24 (3-inch) circles with a biscuit cutter. Press dough circles into each muffin cup. Bake 25 minutes; remove pan from oven and set aside to cool.

In a medium bowl, thoroughly combine cheeses, mayonnaise, pimientos, jalapeños, onion, garlic, and pecans. Fill mini pie crusts with cheese mixture. Serve.

FRIED SQUASH

SERVES 8

....

Some of my favorite childhood memories are of time spent processing fresh vegetables straight from the garden in my grandmother's little kitchen. My mother and grandmother would put up frozen squash all summer long. Some summers I prayed the squash would quit growing so I could just go outside and play instead of having to help bag and freeze. One of the most common refrains I heard after processing was, "Now, let's fry up a pan of squash." That meant we were thankfully done for the day. Equally great for weeknights and summers at the lake, this treat is packed with rich flavor and sweet onions in a crunchy, savory package.

5 cups oil, for frying

3 cups buttermilk

3 pounds yellow summer squash, sliced 1/4-inch thick

1 large Vidalia onion, thinly sliced

3 cups all-purpose flour

1/2 cup cornmeal

2 teaspoons salt

2 teaspoons freshly ground black pepper

Heat oil in a cast iron skillet over medium heat.

Pour buttermilk into a medium bowl and soak squash and onion for 5 minutes.

Combine flour, cornmeal, salt, and pepper in a paper bag. Shake to combine.

Working in small batches, remove squash and onion from buttermilk and place in flour mixture. Shake bag to coat squash well. Add squash and onion to hot oil and cook until golden brown. Cook in batches. Remove squash and onion from oil and drain on paper towels. Serve immediately.

ALL-AMERICAN PIE SHOOTERS

MAKES 12 SHOOTERS

....

Festive, fluffy, and filled with the creamiest, most delicious concoction of powdered sugar, cream cheese, and heavy whipping cream, this dessert is equal parts decadent and patriotic.

    1 recipe SB Pie Dough (page 17)

    2 cups heavy cream

    8 ounces cream cheese, softened

    1 cup powdered sugar

    1 teaspoon vanilla

    1 tablespoon lemon juice

    1/2 teaspoon lemon zest

    1 quart fresh strawberries, diced

    1 quart fresh blueberries

Preheat oven to 400 degrees. Line a baking sheet with parchment paper.

Roll out dough into a 12-inch circle. Using a 1 1/2-inch star cookie cutter, cut 24 small stars. Place stars on baking sheet and bake for 12–15 minutes. Remove from oven and set aside to cool.

Beat cream in a mixer until soft peaks form. Set aside.

In a clean mixing bowl, beat cream cheese and sugar until fluffy. Beat in vanilla, lemon juice, and zest. Whisk half of the whipped cream mixture into cream cheese mixture by hand. Then gently fold in remaining whipped cream.

Crumble up 12 stars and fill the bottom of 12 shot glasses. Pipe cream mixture on top of crumbs. Top with berries, another layer of cream mixture, and garnish with a star.

Note: If you don't have a decorator's piping bag, you can use a ziplock bag. Just fill the bag with whipped cream, squeeze out excess air, cut off 1 corner of the bag, and then pipe the cream.

AUGUST
Girls' Night Treats

As much as I love to pamper my friends and family on special holidays, I also like to take time for myself every once-in-awhile. That's why I love planning a special night to get together with my best girlfriends over wine and, of course, pie. My favorite nights are potluck-style parties, because I feel like you can learn so much about your friends by the foods they make to share with others. The recipes in this chapter are some my favorite guilty pleasures—perfect for sharing with friends.

Squash, Caramelized Onion, and Bacon Pie

Savory Beef Hand Pies

Late Summer Vegetable Tart

Sweet Cream Tart

Sticky Toffee Pudding Pie with Rum Glaze

Simple Blueberry Crostata

SQUASH, CARAMELIZED ONION, AND BACON PIE

SERVES 8

....

My mom used to make a dish with squash, bacon, and caramelized onions, and it was so good that I just had to make my own version. This rich, heavenly pie is one you'll want to make time and again.

    1 recipe SB Pie Dough (page 17)
    2 tablespoons butter
    2 Vidalia onions, thinly sliced
    5 slices bacon
    8 small yellow summer squash, sliced into 1/4-inch rounds
    1/2 teaspoon salt
    1 teaspoon freshly ground black pepper
    1 egg
    1/4 cup sour cream
    1 1/2 cups grated Gruyère cheese

Roll out dough into a 12-inch circle. Place into a 9-inch round pie plate and flute; partially bake the dough (see page 20).

Preheat oven to 375 degrees.

Melt the butter in a medium sauté pan. Add onions and sauté for 40 minutes on medium-low heat, or until onions are caramelized.

Cook bacon in a large sauté pan until crisp. Remove from pan and drain on a paper towel; let cool and then break into pieces. Reserve 2 tablespoons of bacon grease in the pan. Add squash, salt, and pepper to pan and cook for 20 minutes on medium-high heat, stirring occasionally.

In a large bowl, whisk the egg and sour cream to combine. Add bacon, onions, squash, and cheese. Stir to combine. Spoon mixture into pie crust and bake for 25 minutes until golden and bubbly.

SAVORY BEEF HAND PIES

MAKES 8 HAND PIES

These hardy meat hand pies are reminiscent of Old English recipes that have endured for centuries. With creamy, decadent goodness, such as mashed potatoes and cream cheese packed inside a grab-and-go size, these little pies will be gobbled up quickly.

2 tablespoons butter

1 Vidalia onion, sliced

1 egg

1 tablespoon water

1 cup cooked ground chuck

1 cup mashed potatoes

8 ounces cream cheese, softened

1/2 cup frozen peas, thawed

1/2 cup cut frozen carrots, thawed

1 tablespoon chopped fresh parsley

1 teaspoon Worcestershire sauce

1/2 teaspoon salt

1 teaspoon freshly ground black pepper, plus extra

2 recipes SB Pie Dough (page 17)

Preheat oven to 400 degrees. Line a baking sheet with parchment paper.

Melt butter in sauté pan. Add the onion and cook over medium-low heat for about 40 minutes, or until caramelized. Set aside.

Whisk together the egg and water in a small bowl to make an egg wash. Set aside.

In a medium bowl, combine the meat, onions, potatoes, cream cheese, peas, carrots, parsley, Worcestershire sauce, salt, and pepper.

Roll out dough into 2 (12-inch) circles and cut 4 (5 1/2-inch) circles out of each dough circle. Reroll the scraps if needed to get 8 circles.

Brush the edges of the circles with egg wash. Spoon filling into the middle of each dough circle. Fold dough over filling and crimp to seal using your finger or the tines of a fork. Transfer hand pies to baking sheet. Brush the tops with remaining egg wash and sprinkle with pepper. Bake for 25 minutes, or until golden brown.

LATE SUMMER
VEGETABLE TART

SERVES 8

....

*My mother-in-law, Sandy, often served this dish to friends and family on sunset cruises
around Lake Burton. Cut into small pieces and serve on appetizer plates for a vegetarian
treat everyone will enjoy.*

1 recipe SB Pie Dough (page 17)

1 Vidalia onion, sliced

1 red bell pepper, cut into strips

4 tablespoons olive oil, divided

8 cloves garlic, finely chopped, divided

1 small eggplant, peeled and sliced into thin rounds

1/2 teaspoon salt, divided

1 teaspoon freshly ground black pepper, divided

3 tomatoes, sliced

2 large zucchini, sliced

1 tablespoon chopped fresh parsley

1 tablespoon chopped fresh thyme

4 ounces goat cheese, crumbled

Preheat oven to 325 degrees.

Roll out dough into a 9 x 12-inch rectangle. Press into an 8 x 11 1/2-inch rectangular tart
pan. Place in freezer to chill while you prepare the tart filling.

In a large heavy skillet, sauté onion and bell pepper in 2 tablespoons oil for 10 minutes.
Add half the garlic and sauté for 1 minute.

Cover bottom of tart crust with mixture and arrange eggplant evenly over top; sprinkle
with 1/4 teaspoon salt and 1/2 teaspoon pepper. Layer the tomatoes and zucchini over the
eggplant in alternating rows, overlapping slightly. Sprinkle remaining salt and pepper,
herbs, and remaining garlic over top. Drizzle with remaining oil.

Bake, uncovered, for 1 hour, or until veggies are tender. Remove from oven and top with
cheese. Bake 5 more minutes, or until cheese melts.

SWEET CREAM TART

There's absolutely nothing not to love about this creamy, custardy, vanilla tart. Simple and elegant, this dessert is perfect for a ladies' night.

I recipe SB Pie Dough (page 17)
9 egg yolks
I cup granulated sugar
I 1/2 envelopes gelatin
3/4 cups cold water
3 cups heavy cream, whipped
2 teaspoons vanilla
1/2 cup sliced almonds
2 ounces bittersweet chocolate curls

Roll out dough into a 12-inch circle. Place into a 10 1/4-inch tart pan; prebake the dough (see page 20).

Beat egg yolks in a mixer until light. Add sugar and mix well. Soften gelatin in water and then place in a small saucepan and bring to a boil over low heat. Slowly stir gelatin into egg mixture. Fold in whipped cream. Add vanilla and stir gently just to combine.

Cool mixture until it is thick enough to mound slightly. Spoon into tart shell and chill until firm, 3–4 hours.

Garnish with almonds and chocolate curls, to serve.

STICKY TOFFEE PUDDING PIE
WITH RUM GLAZE

SERVES 8

Sure to please even the sweetest of sweet tooths, this pie is the ooey, gooey dessert you didn't know you needed. Kick it up a notch by incorporating a little extra rum in your glaze and use the unique poking technique for an ultra-moist finish. Serve with homemade vanilla ice cream for total perfection.

PIE
1 recipe SB Pie Dough
   (page 17)
3/4 pound dates, pitted
   and chopped
1 1/2 cups water
1 teaspoon baking soda
8 tablespoons unsalted butter,
   room temperature
1/3 cup granulated sugar
2 eggs

1 teaspoon vanilla
1 1/4 cups all-purpose flour
1 teaspoon kosher salt
1 1/2 tablespoons baking powder

GLAZE
10 tablespoons unsalted butter
3/4 cup brown sugar
1/2 cup heavy cream
1/4 teaspoon kosher salt
2 tablespoons good rum

PIE

Roll out dough into a 12-inch circle. Place into a 9-inch round pie plate and flute; prebake the dough (see page 20).

Preheat oven to 375 degrees.

Bring the dates and water to boil in a saucepan over medium-high heat. Once boiling, allow to simmer for 2 minutes and then remove from heat. Stir in baking soda. Set aside.

In a mixer, cream butter and sugar together on high until light and fluffy. With the mixer on low, slowly add eggs, 1 at a time, then add the vanilla. Slowly add the flour and salt. Then slowly add the dates and cooking liquid. Once well-combined, add the baking powder and stir by hand. Pour the batter into the pie crust. Bake for 40 minutes.

GLAZE

Combine the butter, brown sugar, cream, and salt in a medium saucepan and bring to a boil. Reduce heat and simmer for 1 minute. Remove from heat and stir in rum. Set aside.

Poke holes all over the pie with a dinner fork. Pour $^{3}/_{4}$ of the glaze over the pie while still warm and allow to absorb for 30 minutes. Reserve remaining glaze and heat just before serving. Drizzle warm glaze over each slice of pie.

SIMPLE BLUEBERRY CROSTATA

SERVES 6 TO 8

There is nothing more delectable than a fresh fruit crostata. You get more crust than filling. And since the crust is my favorite part, I'm in heaven each time I take a bite of this sweet dessert.

CROSTATA
1 recipe SB Pie Dough (page 17)
3 1/2 cups fresh blueberries
1 1/2 tablespoons all-purpose flour
1 tablespoon granulated sugar
Zest and juice from 1 large lemon

CRUMB TOPPING
1/4 cup all-purpose flour
1/4 cup granulated sugar
4 tablespoons butter

CROSTATA

Preheat oven to 375 degrees. Line a baking sheet with parchment paper.

Roll out dough into a 12-inch circle. Place onto baking sheet.

In a large bowl combine blueberries, flour, sugar, zest, and juice; mix thoroughly. Pour the blueberry mixture into the center of the dough, making a mound and leaving a 1 1/2-inch border around the edge of the dough.

CRUMB TOPPING

In a small bowl, combine the flour, sugar, and butter together using a pastry blender or fork. Evenly crumble the topping mixture over the blueberries.

Fold the dough up over the edge of the blueberries, pinching to create pleats. Bake for 20–25 minutes, or until crust is golden brown.

SEPTEMBER
End of Summer Picnic

We all love summer—the long, sunny days and nights spent catching fireflies in bare feet—but it has to end sometime. That's why I like to savor the last of the season with an outdoor family picnic in September. The recipes in this chapter are all great picnic treats, easily portable family favorites packed with flavor. They're all fairly simple to prepare, so you can focus less on the food and more on your fellowship.

Tabasco Fried Chicken

Homemade Buttermilk Ranch Dressing

Dill Pickles

Fried Green Tomatoes

Herbed Roasted Veggie Salad

Strawberry-Rhubarb Mini Pies

Frozen Lemonade Pie

TABASCO FRIED CHICKEN

SERVES 10

Everyone in the South grows up eating fried chicken, and I'm no exception. Learning to make fried chicken properly is a Southern rite of passage. Though my mom cooked it at least once a week, my mother-in-law completely transformed my view of the dish when she suggested adding a splash or two of Tabasco sauce to some buttermilk and then soaking the chicken before frying. The hint of spice and the creamy buttermilk make all the difference in the world. This is, hands down, the best fried chicken I've ever had.

2 cups buttermilk

3 tablespoons Tabasco sauce

2 whole chickens, cut into pieces

5 cups oil

7 cups all-purpose flour

2 tablespoons garlic powder

2 teaspoons paprika

2 teaspoons cayenne pepper

1 tablespoon kosher salt

2 tablespoons freshly ground black pepper

Homemade Buttermilk Ranch Dressing (page 139)

Combine the buttermilk and Tabasco in large bowl. Add chicken to the buttermilk and soak for 2 hours in the refrigerator.

Remove chicken from the refrigerator and let set for 30 minutes. Frying cold chicken will lower the temperature of the oil and cause the chicken to have a soggy crust.

Fill a large cast iron skillet with oil and heat over medium heat to 350 degrees.

Add the flour, garlic powder, paprika, cayenne, salt, and pepper to a brown paper bag and shake to combine. Working in small batches, add chicken pieces to the flour mixture and shake to completely coat. Add floured chicken to skillet and cook until golden brown, about 15 minutes. Internal temperature should read 170 degrees.

Drain cooked chicken on wire cooling rack and then serve immediately with ranch dressing for dipping.

HOMEMADE BUTTERMILK RANCH DRESSING

MAKES 2 1/2 CUPS

Some things in life shouldn't change. My mother's recipe for ranch dressing is one of them. It's so good you'll want to dip absolutely everything in it. It's versatile enough to be just as good on fried chicken as it is on salad, potatoes, veggies, pizza, and everything in between.

1 cup mayonnaise

1/4 cup sour cream

1 cup buttermilk

2 tablespoons chopped fresh chives

2 tablespoons chopped fresh parsley

1/4 teaspoon soy sauce

2 teaspoons freshly ground black pepper

1/2 teaspoon kosher salt

1 clove garlic, grated

1 teaspoon dried onion

Whisk all ingredients together in a bowl. Refrigerate in a covered jar for up to 2 weeks.

DILL PICKLES

MAKE 4 PINTS

This recipe is one that's been passed down from Mrs. McDonald, a cherished family friend. The perfect pairing for fried chicken, these pickles have a strong bite and are best served cold. Any leftover juice can be saved to pour over pasta or potato salad for an extra layer of unexpected flavor.

3 cups white vinegar

3 cups water

1/3 cup salt

4 cups sliced cucumbers, chilled

2 tablespoons dill seeds

In a large saucepan, bring the vinegar, water, and salt to a boil; boil for 2–3 minutes.

Remove from heat and completely cool.

Loosely pack the cucumbers into 4 pint-size Mason jars. Evenly distribute the dill seeds between the jars.

Pour cooled vinegar mixture over the cucumbers and seal with jar lids. Store in a cool dark area. Wait 2–3 months before eating.

Note: Keeping the cucumbers in the refrigerator until you are ready to fill the jars ensures the pickles will be crisp.

FRIED GREEN TOMATOES

SERVES 8

Somehow I made it all the way to adulthood without ever having prepared this classic, Southern staple. Poor Alex had to be the guinea pig for all of my first attempts at it after we were married. Fortunately, with time, I found just the right recipe. I think we're all better off for it. Drizzle these with Homemade Buttermilk Ranch Dressing (page 139) for out-of-this-world flavor.

3 cups vegetable oil

3 cups buttermilk

6 fresh green tomatoes, sliced into 1/2-inch-thick slices

3 cups all-purpose flour

1 cup fresh ground cornmeal

1 teaspoon salt

2 teaspoons freshly ground black pepper

1/2 teaspoon paprika

1/2 teaspoon cayenne pepper

1 teaspoon garlic powder

Heat oil to 350 degrees in a large cast iron skillet over medium heat.

Pour buttermilk into a medium bowl and soak tomatoes slices for 5 minutes.

Combine flour, cornmeal, salt, pepper, paprika, cayenne, and garlic powder in a large bowl. Stir to combine. Working in small batches, dredge tomato slices in flour mixture, add to hot oil, and cook until golden brown on both sides. Remove and drain on cooling rack. Serve immediately.

Note: If you don't have a thermometer, test the oil by sprinkling in a little cornmeal. If it sizzles when it hits the oil, it is ready.

HERBED ROASTED
VEGGIE SALAD

SERVES 8 TO 10

This well-textured salad is everything I look for in a late summer dish. Reminiscent of a succotash salad, and loaded with brightly colored vegetables, this robust dish's sweet, herby vinaigrette will leave you feeling light.

1 1/2 cups fresh or frozen lima beans

1 1/2 cups fresh or frozen shelled edamame

1 pound haricots verts, halved

1 cup fresh corn kernels

1 clove garlic, minced

1/4 cup finely diced scallions

2 tablespoons olive oil

1 teaspoon kosher salt, plus extra

1/2 teaspoon freshly ground black pepper, plus extra

1 cup chopped fresh tomatoes

3 tablespoons chopped fresh basil

2 tablespoons chopped fresh parsley

1 1/2 tablespoons red wine vinegar

1 teaspoon honey

1 teaspoon lime zest

2 tablespoons lime juice

Preheat oven to 400 degrees.

Combine the lima beans, edamame, haricots verts, corn, garlic, scallions, oil, 1 teaspoon salt, and 1/2 teaspoon pepper in a bowl and toss together. Spread evenly over a large baking sheet. Roast for 20 minutes, stirring occasionally to make sure the beans don't burn. Remove from oven and transfer to a large bowl.

In a small bowl, mix together the tomatoes, basil, parsley, vinegar, honey, zest, and juice. Add to the bean mixture. Toss to combine. Season with salt and pepper, to taste.

STRAWBERRY-RHUBARB MINI PIES

This recipe is in memory of my great-great grandfather, Jim Carpenter, whose signature dish was a double-crust rhubarb pie. He grew rhubarb in his backyard garden, watching over it diligently as he waited for it to yield the tart vegetable that made his pie the star that it was. This miniature twist on Grandpa's classic is a late-summer recipe perfect for an outdoor picnic. You can pack these individual portions and pass them out to kids and adults alike while watching the sunset.

2 recipes SB Pie Dough (page 17)
2 $1/2$ cups sliced rhubarb, ($1/2$-inch slices)
2 $1/2$ cups sliced fresh strawberries, ($1/2$-inch slices)
1 cup plus 2 tablespoons granulated sugar, divided
$1/3$ cup all-purpose flour
1 $1/4$ teaspoons orange zest
2 tablespoons butter, cubed
$1/4$ cup heavy cream

Preheat oven to 400 degrees.

Roll out dough into 2 (12-inch) circles. Cut both circles into $1/2$-inch wide strips.

Mix the rhubarb, strawberries, 1 cup sugar, flour, and zest together in a large bowl.

Pour mixture into 6 individual au gratin dishes and dot with butter. Lattice the top of each pie with dough (see page 23). Brush tops of each pie with cream and sprinkle with remaining sugar.

Bake for 15 minutes. Then lower oven temperature to 350 degrees and bake for 30 minutes until bubbly.

FROZEN LEMONADE PIE

SERVES 8

What sweeter way to end the summer than with a frozen lemonade pie? Creating this fun dessert is the perfect way to get kids involved in the kitchen and start their creative juices flowing as school starts up again. Allow your kids to decorate the top with edible decorations or fresh berries.

1 recipe SB Pie Dough (page 17)
1/2 gallon vanilla ice cream (I prefer High Road Vanilla Fleur Del Sel Ice Cream)
1 (6-ounce) can frozen lemonade concentrate, thawed
Fresh berries, of choice

Roll out dough into a 12-inch circle. Place into a 9-inch pie plate and flute; prebake the dough (see page 20). Place in refrigerator to chill.

Blend ice cream in a mixer until mushy. Add lemonade concentrate and mix thoroughly. Pour into pie crust and place in freezer until frozen. To serve, decorate top with berries.

OCTOBER
Game Day Tailgate

In the South, college football approaches the status of a major religion. Cheering for your favorite SEC (or ACC) team is practically a way of life. Though my husband and I cheer for different teams on game day (Georgia Bulldogs for me, Auburn Tigers for him), we can always count on great food and the camaraderie of a good tailgate to bring us together during the season. All of the food in this chapter is designed to transport beautifully and hold heat well before a game. All you will have to worry about is how your team is doing!

Marinated Chicken Wings

Pineapple Casserole Pie

Old-Fashioned Macaroni Salad

Sloppy Joe Hand Pies

Chili Mac

S'more Pie

MARINATED CHICKEN WINGS

SERVES 8 TO 10

Simple, yet satisfying, these chicken wings can be marinated overnight and grilled the next morning. Although this is a dry wing recipe, that keeps the mess to a minimum, rest assured it doesn't skimp on flavor!

1/4 cup butter

1/4 cup apple cider vinegar

1/2 cup freshly squeezed lemon juice

1/2 teaspoon pepper

2 teaspoons kosher salt

1/2 teaspoon thyme

1 teaspoon onion salt

3 to 5 pounds chicken wings

Combine the butter, vinegar, juice, pepper, salt, thyme, and onion salt in small saucepan. Stir and heat over medium-high heat, bringing almost to a boil. Remove from heat, and set aside.

Place chicken in a large ziplock bag. Pour marinade over chicken, seal bag, shake to coat, and refrigerate overnight.

Preheat grill to 350 degrees.

Remove chicken from refrigerator and place wings directly on the grill. Grill for 25 minutes, or until cooked through, turning wings every 5–7 minutes.

PINEAPPLE CASSEROLE PIE

SERVES 8

If you've ever had a pineapple casserole in the South, you will forever remember the taste. The mixture of sweet pineapple and rich, gooey cheese is unexpectedly delicious. I love this dish for fall and football season because it travels beautifully, and is wonderful served at room temperature.

1 recipe SB Pie Dough (page 17)

2 (20-ounce) cans chunked pineapple

5 tablespoons all-purpose flour

3/4 cup granulated sugar

1 1/2 cups grated sharp cheddar cheese

1 sleeve Ritz crackers, crushed

4 tablespoons butter, melted

Roll out dough into a 12-inch circle. Place into a 9-inch pie plate and flute; prebake the dough (see page 20).

Preheat oven to 350 degrees.

Drain pineapple, reserving 1/2 cup juice. Combine flour, sugar, and pineapple in a bowl and toss to coat. Layer pineapple mixture and cheese in pie crust. Pour reserved pineapple juice over the filling. Sprinkle crushed crackers over the top and pour the butter over the crackers. Bake for 40 minutes until lightly browned.

OLD-FASHIONED MACARONI SALAD

SERVES 6 TO 8

My sweet granddaddy was a huge fan of macaroni salad. His wife, my Mama Betty, still makes it every single summer for family gatherings at the lake. As an adult, I often make her recipe for tailgates because it travels so well. Besides, who doesn't love a good old Southern macaroni salad?

1 pound elbow macaroni

3 hardboiled eggs, chopped

1/2 cup pimientos, drained

1 cup mayonnaise

2 tablespoons yellow mustard

3 stalks celery, chopped

4 green onions, chopped

2 tablespoons sweet pickle relish

1/2 teaspoon granulated sugar

Kosher salt, to taste

Freshly ground black pepper, to taste

Cook macaroni according to package directions. Drain and set aside.

In a large bowl, combine eggs, pimientos, mayonnaise, mustard, celery, onions, relish, and sugar; mix well. Add macaroni to the bowl and toss to coat. Season with salt and pepper. Chill before serving.

SLOPPY JOE HAND PIES

MAKES 5 HAND PIES

I like to make these in the shape of little footballs. They're always a touchdown with friends and family at tailgate parties.

1 pound ground chuck
1 onion, chopped
2 tablespoons yellow mustard
1/2 teaspoon salt
1/2 teaspoon freshly ground black pepper
2 tablespoons Worcestershire sauce
1/2 cup ketchup
2 recipes SB Pie Dough (page 17)

Preheat oven to 400 degrees. Line a baking sheet with parchment paper.

Place the meat and onion in a large skillet. Cook, breaking up meat with a spoon until it is no longer pink and the onions are softened. Drain excess grease from meat. Add the mustard, salt, pepper, Worcestershire sauce, and ketchup and simmer for 20 minutes. Remove from heat and set aside to cool.

Roll out dough into 2 (12-inch) circles. Cut 5 hand-size football shapes out of each circle for a total of 10 footballs. Reroll the scraps if needed to get all the football shapes. Place 5 football shapes on parchment. Spoon Soppy Joe mix evenly onto each shape. Place remaining 5 football shapes over the mixture and press around the edges to seal closed. Using a sharp knife, cut slits in the top of each football to look like the laces. Bake for 25 minutes, or until golden brown.

CHILI MAC

SERVES 6

....

My kids clean their bowl every time I prepare this dish. It's packed with flavor and hearty protein, making it the perfect tailgate food for adults and children. Transfer to a warm slow cooker for easy transport.

1 teaspoon olive oil

1 medium onion, chopped

3 pounds ground chuck

2 (8-ounce) cans tomato sauce

1 (6-ounce) can tomato paste

1 (14.5-ounce) can diced tomatoes

3 tablespoons Worcestershire sauce

3 tablespoons chili powder

1 tablespoon salt

1 tablespoon black pepper

1/2 tablespoon garlic powder

2 (14.5-ounce) cans red kidney beans, drained

2 (4-ounce) cans mushrooms, drained

1 (16-ounce) package elbow macaroni, cooked and drained

Sour cream, sliced scallions, and grated cheese, optional

Place the oil in a 6-quart Dutch oven and sauté the onion until softened. Add the meat and cook, breaking up with a spoon until no longer pink. Add tomato sauce, tomato paste, tomatoes, Worcestershire sauce, chili powder, salt, pepper, and garlic powder; stir to combine. Let simmer for 2 hours, stirring occasionally.

Stir in the beans, mushrooms, and pasta and continue to simmer for 15 more minutes. Serve with sour cream, scallions, and cheese if desired.

S'MORE PIE

SERVES 8

....

Nothing makes me think of fall quite like s'mores. Just the word conjures up memories of late-fall bonfires and melty, chocolaty goodness. This pie satisfies all those cravings, and more, with its rich silky filling and fluffy, marshmallow cream topping. One bite and you'll be in cool-weather heaven. No coat hangers or ashes needed!

CRUST

1 recipe SB Pie Dough (page 17)

4 ounces bittersweet chocolate, finely chopped

FILLING

1/3 cup granulated sugar

1/3 cup unsweetened cocoa powder

2 tablespoons cornstarch

1/8 teaspoon salt

1 3/4 cups whole milk, divided

1/4 cup heavy whipping cream

4 ounces bittersweet chocolate, finely chopped

1 teaspoon vanilla

GRAHAM CRACKER CRUMBS

3 1/4 cups crushed graham crackers

1 1/2 cups butter, melted

1 1/2 cups brown sugar

1 teaspoon vanilla

1/8 teaspoon ground cinnamon

1/8 teaspoon ground nutmeg

TOPPING

3 egg whites

1 (7-ounce) jar marshmallow crème

CRUST

Roll out dough into a 12-inch circle. Place into a 9-inch round pie plate and flute; prebake the dough (see page 20). Remove from oven and sprinkle chocolate over bottom of hot crust. Let melt until chocolate is soft, 1–2 minutes and spread evenly over crust. Place in refrigerator and chill until chocolate sets, about 30 minutes.

FILLING

Combine sugar, cocoa, cornstarch, and salt in a heavy saucepan and whisk over medium heat. Gradually add 1/3 cup milk, whisking until a smooth paste forms. Whisk in remaining milk and the cream. Stir mixture over medium heat until pudding thickens and begins to bubble around the edges, about 5 minutes. Add chocolate and stir until melted and mixture is smooth. Remove from heat and add vanilla. Pour into pie crust.

GRAHAM CRACKER CRUMBS

Combine all ingredients in a bowl and mix. Reserve 2 tablespoons of mixture. Crumble graham cracker mixture over chocolate filling. Place pie in refrigerator and chill overnight.

TOPPING

Preheat oven to 400 degrees.

Beat egg whites on high speed with electric mixer until stiff peaks form. Beat 1/4 of the marshmallow crème into mixture; repeat 3 times, beating until smooth. Spread over cracker crumbs and filling. Bake 8 minutes, or until meringue is browned. Sprinkle top with reserved graham cracker mixture.

NOVEMBER
After Thanksgiving Bites

Thanksgiving is the busiest and most exciting holiday of the year at Southern Baked Pie Company. Our bakery works twenty-four hours a day, starting the first of November. Our teams produce thousands of pies for our pie shops, making each by hand. We ship pies all over for families near and far to enjoy. As you can imagine, we are all exhausted on Thanksgiving Eve.

Thankfully, my precious mother has taken on the role of preparing the Thanksgiving meal. My contribution is, of course, pie! Thanksgiving is such a beautiful, special holiday, but it always presents a challenge—what to do with all the food that's leftover. After stuffing ourselves with enough holiday fare to last through the end of the year, my family doesn't usually want to see another piece of turkey for a while, let alone eat one. But I'm no fan of waste; so a few years ago I started experimenting with ways to repurpose Thanksgiving foods into new, delicious dishes that will have everyone clamoring to eat them again. These recipes are designed to be bite-size, snack-friendly, and out-of-this-world.

Hot Bacon and Cheddar Dip

Cranberry Chutney Pie Pick-Ups

Wedge Salad with Roquefort Dressing

Turkey Pot Pies

Meatless Mincemeat Pie

Roasted Sweet Potato Pie with Pecan Streusel

HOT BACON AND CHEDDAR DIP

SERVES 8 TO 10

This is one of my absolute favorite appetizers. It's also great for munching on throughout the day as you catch-up with friends and family and watch your favorite college football games.

16 ounces cream cheese, softened

1 cup mayonnaise

2 cups grated sharp cheddar cheese

1/2 cup chopped green onions

3 pounds bacon, crisp cooked and crumbled

12 to 15 finely crushed butter crackers

Crostini crackers

Preheat oven to 350 degrees.

Beat the cream cheese in a bowl until smooth and fluffy. Add the mayonnaise, cheese, scallions, and 1/2 of the bacon; mix well. Spoon the mixture into a baking dish and sprinkle with the remaining bacon and crackers.

Bake for 15–20 minutes, or until brown and bubbly. Serve warm with crostini crackers.

CRANBERRY CHUTNEY PIE PICK-UPS

MAKES 24 PICK-UPS

We traditionally have cranberry chutney instead of cranberry sauce at Thanksgiving. These scrumptious little bites are a great way to use up the leftover chutney. I guarantee no one will complain about seeing it again.

2 recipes SB Pie Dough (page 17)
2 cups cranberries
1/2 cup water
1 small onion, sliced
1 cup granulated sugar
1/4 teaspoon ground ginger
1/4 teaspoon ground cinnamon
1/8 teaspoon allspice
1/8 teaspoon salt
1 (8-ounce) can pineapple tidbits, drained
1/2 cup chopped pecans
8 ounces cream cheese, softened
2 tablespoons chopped fresh parsley

Preheat oven to 375 degrees. Line a baking sheet with parchment paper.

Roll out dough into 2 (12-inch) circles. Cut out 24 (3-inch) circles using a cookie cutter with a scalloped or decorative edge. Place circles on baking sheet and prick using the times of a fork. Bake for 15 minutes. Remove from oven to cool; set aside.

Combine cranberries, water, onion, sugar, ginger, cinnamon, allspice, and salt in a saucepan. Cook over medium heat, uncovered, for 10–15 minutes, or until cranberry skins pop. Stir in pineapple and pecans. Reduce heat to low and cook an additional 30 minutes, stirring often. Remove from heat and set aside to cool.

To serve, spoon cream cheese over circles and top with a dollop of cranberry mixture. Garnish with parsley.

WEDGE SALAD WITH ROQUEFORT DRESSING

MAKES 4 SERVINGS

This simple salad is a terrific accompaniment to all the Thanksgiving leftovers.

1 large head iceberg lettuce

1 cup full-fat sour cream

1/4 pound Roquefort cheese, crumbled

1 1/2 teaspoons lemon juice

1/4 teaspoon dry mustard

1/4 teaspoon pepper

1/4 teaspoon Tabasco sauce

1/2 cup buttermilk

1 cup halved grape tomatoes

4 slices bacon, cooked and crumbled

1 shallot, thinly sliced

Slice lettuce into 4 wedges. Place each wedge in individual serving bowls.

Mix the sour cream, cheese, lemon juice, mustard, pepper, Tabasco, and buttermilk together in a small bowl until combined. Drizzle the dressing evenly over lettuce wedges and top with tomatoes, bacon, and shallot.

TURKEY POT PIES

SERVES 4

Everyone is usually a bit burned out on turkey by the day after Thanksgiving. Still, this pie is a great way to repurpose your leftovers and finish them off quickly. The creamy gravy keeps the turkey from going dry, and the comforting pastry makes everyone want to dig in for bite after bite.

1 recipe SB Pie Dough (page 17)
8 tablespoons (1 stick) butter
1/2 cup all-purpose flour
4 cups turkey or chicken stock
4 cups cubed cooked turkey
1/4 teaspoon dried sage
1/4 teaspoon dried thyme
1/2 cup diced carrots
1/2 cup green peas
1 cup pearl onions
1/4 cup heavy cream
1/2 teaspoon freshly ground black pepper
1/2 teaspoon kosher salt

Preheat oven to 400 degrees.

Roll out dough into a 12-inch circle. Cut 4 (5-inch) circles out of dough. Cut each circle into 1/2-inch strips. Set aside.

In a saucepan, melt butter over medium heat. Add flour and whisk for 3–5 minutes, allowing flour to cook. Add stock and whisk to combine; bring to a simmer and cook for 5 minutes. Add the turkey, sage, thyme, carrots, peas, and onions. Remove from stove and divide filling equally among 4 oven-safe ramekins or small Dutch ovens. Top filling with strips of dough in a lattice weave pattern (see page 23). Brush with cream and sprinkle with pepper and salt.

Bake for 15 minutes. Reduce heat to 350 degrees and bake for 45 minutes, or until crust is golden brown and filling is bubbling. If the crust starts to burn, lightly cover with aluminum foil and continue baking.

MEATLESS MINCEMEAT PIE

A lot of people love this holiday classic, but it's not made very often anymore. This meatless version of mincemeat pie incorporates all the spices and fruits that spring to mind when you imagine Thanksgiving.

3 recipes SB Pie Dough (page 17)

3 large apples, peeled, cored, and cut into 1/2-inch cubes

1/2 cup freshly squeezed orange juice

3 tablespoons fresh orange zest

1/2 cup brown sugar

1 cup golden raisins

1/2 cup dried apricots, chopped

1/4 teaspoon salt

1/4 teaspoon ground cinnamon

1/4 teaspoon ground nutmeg

1/4 teaspoon ground cloves

1/2 cup chopped walnuts

1 1/2 teaspoons vanilla

2 tablespoons brandy

1/4 cup heavy cream

2 tablespoons turbinado sugar

Roll out dough into 3 (12-inch) circles. Line a (9-inch) pie plate with 1 circle of dough. Place pie plate and remaining dough in the refrigerator.

Combine the apples, juice, zest, brown sugar, raisins, apricots, salt, and spices in a medium saucepan. Cover and simmer over low heat for 25–30 minutes.

Remove the lid and continue simmering until the liquid evaporates. Stir in the walnuts, vanilla, and brandy; remove from heat and let cool. Spread cooled mixture evenly over the dough in the pie plate.

Remove remaining dough from refrigerator, let come to room temperature, and cut into 1/2-inch-thick strips. Lattice weave (see page 23) the 2 strips together to form the top crust. Place lattice top over pie, flute edges, and place in the freezer for 1 hour.

Preheat oven to 400 degrees.

Remove pie from freezer and brush the top with cream; sprinkle with sugar.

Bake in lower third of oven for 15 minutes. Reduce heat to 350 degrees and bake for 45 minutes, or until golden.

ROASTED SWEET POTATO PIE WITH PECAN STREUSEL

SERVES 8

....

Growing up I always requested that my grandmother make me a sweet potato pie at Thanksgiving with just a smidge of sweet potato filling. I was far more interested in the crust than the filling. This recipe, introduced to me by my mother-in-law, Sandy, reverses that craving. The filling here is melt-in-your-mouth perfection, and not too spicy. I like to use Washington Red sweet potatoes because they give the sweetest, most tender flavor.

FILLING
1 recipe SB Pie Dough
   (page 17)
5 medium sweet potatoes
1/3 cup dark brown sugar
3 tablespoons butter, melted
2 eggs
1 teaspoon ground cinnamon

1/2 teaspoon pumpkin pie spice
1/4 teaspoon ground cloves
1/8 teaspoon ground nutmeg

TOPPING
1/2 cup dark brown sugar
1/3 cup all-purpose flour
3/4 cup chopped pecans
1/3 cup butter, melted

Preheat oven to 350 degrees.

Roll out dough into a 12-inch circle. Place into a 9-inch round pie plate and flute. Set aside.

FILLING

Roast unpeeled sweet potatoes until tender. Remove from oven and let cool. When cooled and easy to handle, peel potatoes, place in a large bowl, and mash. Add the brown sugar, butter, eggs, cinnamon, pumpkin pie spice, cloves, and nutmeg and mix well to thoroughly combine. Spoon mixture into the pie crust.

TOPPING

Mix the brown sugar, flour, and pecans together in a bowl. Add the butter and mix to combine. Sprinkle evenly over pie filling.

Lower oven temperature to 325 degrees and bake pie in lower third of oven for 45 minutes.

DECEMBER
Holiday Dishes

When I was a little girl my family spent every Christmas Eve at Lake Burton with my Aunt Betty Jeanne and Uncle Bob. As much as I loved Christmas Day, it was always Christmas Eve I found myself looking forward to the most. Every year we'd have a big, formal black-tie party to celebrate the Christmas season, and I'd stuff myself with all the holiday goodies my mom, aunt, and grandmother, Betty, had whipped up in the kitchen.

In recent years, I've been lucky enough to pass this tradition on to my own family. By Christmas Eve, the holiday pie-frenzy at Southern Baked has quieted and I'm able to take the day off and spend it in the kitchen with my family, reconnecting and cooking the recipes that I have loved all my life. The recipes in this chapter represent some of my favorite traditions, and I hope you'll love them every bit as much as I do.

Standing Rib Roast

Spinach Artichoke Pie

Horseradish Mashed Potato Casserole

Spoon-Worthy Egg Nog

Christmas Scramble

Coconut Cream Napoleons

Cranberry-Pear Pie

STANDING RIB ROAST

SERVES 6

A standing rib roast is an old tradition in my husband's family. Since we've been married, I've taken it on. This beautifully-seasoned roast comes out of the oven with a crunchy, delicious crust that the two of us love to snack on before we begin to carve.

5 to 7 pound rib roast

6 cloves garlic, minced

1 tablespoon kosher salt

1 tablespoon freshly ground black pepper

1 tablespoon all-purpose flour

Preheat oven to 450 degrees.

Let meat come to room temperature. Combine garlic, salt, pepper, and flour together in a small bowl. Rub meat completely with garlic mixture. Stand meat on ribs in a roasting pan and place in the oven. Roast for 20 minutes. Reduce temperature to 325 degrees and continue to roast until internal temperature is medium rare (130 degrees) or to your liking, about 90 minutes.

SPINACH ARTICHOKE PIE

SERVES 8

One of Alex's favorite side dishes, I make this every Christmas Eve without fail. Sometimes it's hard to beat the classics—especially when they're warm and full of comforting goodness.

- 1 recipe SB Pie Dough (page 17)
- 2 (6-ounce) jars marinated artichoke hearts, drained
- 2 (10-ounce) packages frozen chopped spinach, thawed and drained
- 8 ounces cream cheese, softened
- 8 tablespoons (1 stick butter), melted
- Dash of lemon juice

Preheat oven to 325 degrees.

Roll out dough into a 12-inch circle. Place into a 9-inch round pie plate and flute.

Spread artichoke hearts in the bottom of the pie crust. In a medium bowl, mix together the spinach, cream cheese, butter, and lemon juice until well-combined; spread over artichoke hearts.

Bake in lower third of oven for 30–35 minutes, or until bubbly.

HORSERADISH MASHED POTATO CASSEROLE

SERVES 6 TO 8

This is one of my favorite dishes from those childhood Christmas Eve parties. The horseradish gives the creamy potatoes the perfect kick. It also happens to pair excellently with the Standing Rib Roast (page 181)—looks like some things are just meant to be.

5 pounds baking potatoes, peeled and cubed

8 ounces cream cheese, room temperature, cut into chunks

8 tablespoons (1 stick) unsalted butter, room temperature

1 cup sour cream, room temperature

3/4 cup heavy cream, heated

1/4 cup milk, heated

1/2 teaspoon salt

1/2 teaspoon freshly ground black pepper, plus extra

3 tablespoons horseradish

2 tablespoons chopped fresh parsley

Preheat oven to 350 degrees. Butter a 9 x 12-inch baking dish and set aside.

Boil potatoes in a large pot until tender; drain. Add the cream cheese, butter, sour cream, cream, milk, salt, pepper, and horseradish. Mash together with a potato masher until smooth and butter has melted. Place in prepared dish and bake for 30 minutes. Garnish with parsley and pepper.

SPOON-WORTHY EGG NOG

SERVES 10

This rich, creamy eggnog is the recipe my Uncle Bob made famous in our large, extended family. My mom asked him to teach her how to make it, and now she always makes it on Christmas Eve. She has graciously passed the recipe down to me. It's a bit of a spin on the traditional version. In fact, it's so thick you have to eat it with a spoon! Nevertheless, it's absolutely divine, and if your holidays are anything like mine, you'll have half the guests asking for the recipe by the end of the night.

6 eggs
1 cup granulated sugar
3/4 cup bourbon
1/4 cup rum
1/4 cup brandy
1 quart heavy cream
Ground nutmeg, to taste
Fresh mint

Separate egg yolks and whites. Beat yolks and sugar together in mixer on medium speed. Add the bourbon, rum, and brandy and continue to mix until well-combined. Set aside.

Whip egg whites in mixer until stiff peaks form. Fold into the egg yolk mixture. Set aside.

Whip cream in mixer until soft peaks form. Fold into egg mixture. Serve immediately, garnished with a sprinkle of nutmeg and fresh mint.

CHRISTMAS SCRAMBLE

Every Christmas, my grandmother Betty allowed me help her make this recipe. I would stand on a chair, because I wasn't tall enough to see over the counter, and mix everything up in a big metal pan. The thing I loved most about cooking with her is that she always let me mix things with my hands. I learned so much about the different textures of foods and the way foods blend together by working with my hands. There is something about getting your hands dirty when cooking that just makes you feel accomplished.

2 cups canola oil

2 tablespoons Worcestershire sauce

1 tablespoon garlic salt

1 tablespoon seasoned salt

2 pounds pecan halves

1 (12-ounce) box bite-size shredded wheat

1 (10-ounce) box Cheerios

6 ounces Rice Chex squares

6 ounces Wheat Chex squares

1 (6-ounce) package pretzel sticks

Preheat oven to 250 degrees.

In a small bowl, mix together the oil, Worcestershire sauce, garlic salt, and seasoned salt.

Mix pecans, cereal, and pretzels together in a large roasting pan and drizzle with oil mixture; stir to coat.

Bake for 2 hours, stirring and turning mixture with wooden spoon every 15 minutes. Be careful not to crush.

COCONUT CREAM NAPOLEONS

I love to get the kids involved with these fun, deconstructed coconut cream pies. Even more, I love that you can make this custard in the microwave instead of mixing it over the hot stove. In my house, easy and delicious is the name of the game, and these definitely fit that bill.

2 recipes SB Pie Dough
  (page 17)
1/3 cup granulated sugar
2 tablespoons cornstarch
1/8 teaspoon salt
1 cup milk
1 egg plus 1 egg yolk, well-beaten

1 tablespoon butter
1 1/4 teaspoons vanilla, divided
1 1/2 cups shredded coconut
1 1/2 cups heavy cream
1/2 cup powdered sugar
1/2 cup toasted coconut

Preheat oven to 375 degrees. Line a baking sheet with parchment paper.

Roll out dough into 2 (12-inch) circles. Cut 6 (3-inch) squares out of each circle for a total of 12. Reroll scraps and cut more squares, if you want. There will be plenty of filling for the extra squares. Place squares on baking sheet and bake for 20 minutes. Remove from oven and set aside.

In a 1-quart glass bowl, blend together the sugar, cornstarch, and salt. Gradually stir in the milk, mixing well. Microwave on high for 5–7 minutes, stirring every 3 minutes, until mixture is smooth and thickened. Stir a small amount of hot pudding quickly into the eggs. Return egg mixture to pudding, mixing well. Microwave at medium high 1–3 minutes, stirring after 1 minute, until smooth and thickened. Add butter, 1 teaspoon vanilla, and shredded coconut. Stir until butter is melted. Let cool or refrigerate until ready to assemble Napoleons.

Whip cream, powdered sugar, and remaining vanilla in a mixer on high speed until stiff peaks form.

To assemble, start by layering a spoonful of custard over half of the baked squares followed by a spoonful of whipped cream. Top each with another square and press gently. Top with a spoonful of custard and then whipped cream. Sprinkle with toasted coconut.

CRANBERRY-PEAR PIE

SERVES 8

Out of all of the recipes I make, this dish tastes the most like Christmas to me. Between the warm spices like cinnamon, cloves, and nutmeg, and the tart cranberries and soft, sweet pears, it has all of the flavors you associate with the holidays. And the best part is I make it with a lattice-top crust that I let my children help me weave together. The pie is a labor of love as much as it is a delicious dessert.

2 recipes SB Pie Dough (page 17)

3 pears, peeled and sliced

3 cups cranberries

3/4 cup granulated sugar

1/2 teaspoon ground cinnamon

1/4 teaspoon ground cloves

1/8 teaspoon ground nutmeg

3 tablespoons all-purpose flour

1 tablespoon cornstarch

Preheat oven to 400 degrees.

Roll out dough into 2 (12-inch) circles. Line a (9-inch) pie plate with 1 circle of dough. Place pie plate and remaining dough in the refrigerator while you prepare the filling.

Mix pears, cranberries, sugar, cinnamon, cloves, nutmeg, flour, and cornstarch in a large bowl, coating the fruit. Spread filling into pie crust.

Cut remaining dough into strips. Lattice weave the strips (see page 23) over the filling; flute edges.

Bake for 15 minutes. Reduce temperature to 350 degrees and bake for 45 minutes, or until golden brown and bubbly.

ACKNOWLEDGMENTS

A cookbook is so much more than pages filled with delicious recipes and stunning photographs. It is also a journey and an adventure; one that is chock-full of stories, memories, long days filled with belly-aching laughter, and countless hours of hard work. Writing this cookbook has been a joy because of the support and guidance I have been blessed with from my family, my friends, and my teams at both Southern Baked Pie Company and Gibbs Smith. This book would not be what it is without each and every one of you.

Special thanks to Gill Autry, my photographer and creative director, who understood my vision without even having to ask. The photographs he captured truly speak my story—no words are needed and that is such a gift.

To Abby Breaux, for capturing the gentle love I have for my two boys, and the fun we have in the kitchen together. Your photographs show the authentic me.

To Maggie Auffarth, for taking my ideas, my stories, and my thoughts and turning them into the loveliest words imaginable. You brought the South that I know and love to life.

To Gena Hood, my Auntie Articulate, for editing this book countless times. You gave me the words I was looking for and made them sound as if they were my own.

To my talented team at Southern Baked Pie Company, you held down the fort in my absence. And Autumn Nyugen, my personal assistant, your belief in me pulled me through this book.

To my friend James Farmer, who believed in me and introduced me to the amazing folks at Gibbs Smith.

To the incomparable team at Gibbs Smith, especially to Madge Braid for believing in me and giving me the opportunity to write my first cookbook, and to Michelle Branson for your guidance and patience with me.

To Sarah Billingsley, my dear friend, for not only opening up her home and allowing me to shoot photos in her gorgeous kitchen, but also for supplying me with the most unique props for styling. Your advice, support, and friendship means the world to me.

To Cathy Auffarth, MaryBeth Wood, Nancy Addison, Dana Gay, and all the sweet friends who shared their silver, dishes, and antiques with me, as well as the friends and family who taste-tested countless recipes and offered feedback.

To the patrons of Southern Baked Pie Company, without your support, none of this would be possible.

To Wanda Dalton, my mother, who lifted me up every day and whose encouragement made this book possible. You are my lifesaver. All my love and admiration to you.

To my mother-in-law Sandy Wilbanks, you taught me to make pie dough and provided me with countless recipes. Your influence over this book is evident on every page. You are such an inspiration to my life.

And finally, to Alex, my husband and most favorite person in the world, thank you for loving me through all the crazy days of stress, and the disasters I created while cooking and photographing in our tiny home. You allow me to shine as you quietly work in the background, bringing my dreams into reality. You are one in a million. Austin, Dalton, and I are so blessed because of you.

Last, but certainly not least, to my two precious boys, Austin and Dalton, who gave up countless hours of my attention and love so I could write and cook for this book. My greatest joy in life is being your mom. I love you.

INDEX

METRIC CONVERSION CHART

VOLUME MEASUREMENTS		WEIGHT MEASUREMENTS		TEMPERATURE CONVERSION	
U.S.	METRIC	U.S.	METRIC	FAHRENHEIT	CELSIUS
1 teaspoon	5 ml	1/2 ounce	15 g	250	120
1 tablespoon	15 ml	1 ounce	30 g	300	150
1/4 cup	60 ml	3 ounces	90 g	325	160
1/3 cup	75 ml	4 ounces	115 g	350	180
1/2 cup	125 ml	8 ounces	225 g	375	190
2/3 cup	150 ml	12 ounces	350 g	400	200
3/4 cup	175 ml	1 pound	450 g	425	220
1 cup	250 ml	2 1/4 pounds	1 kg	450	230

Amanda Wilbanks opened her first retail bakery in Gainesville, Georgia, in 2012. Southern Baked Pie Company now has three retail locations in Georgia and a distribution center for shipping pies across the country. Amanda lives in Gainesville with her husband and two sons.

12/6